GO:
FLEX YOUR STORY POWER

Imparting Life by Sharing Jesus' Love

JIM STERN

Published by Trexo

Houston, Texas

Go: Flex Your Story Power – Imparting Life by Sharing Jesus' Love

© 2021 by Jim Stern

All rights reserved. No portion of this workbook may be reproduced, stored in a retrieval system, or transmitted in any form or by any means—electronic, mechanical, photocopy, recording, scanning, or otherwise, except for brief quotations in critical reviews or articles—without the prior written permission of the publisher.

Published in Houston, Texas, by Trexo.

Unless otherwise indicated, Scripture quotations are taken from the New American Standard Bible®, Copyright © 1960, 1962, 1963, 1968, 1971, 1972, 1973, 1975, 1977, 1995 by The Lockman Foundation. Used by permission.

Scripture quotations marked NIV are taken from the Holy Bible, New International Version®, NIV®. Copyright © 1973, 1978, 1984, 2011 by Biblica, Inc.™ Used by permission of Zondervan. All rights reserved worldwide. www.zondervan.com.

Emphases in Scripture quotations are the author's.

All web addresses were current as of the writing of this book.

To one of my soulmates, Mike Sellars (September 30, 1955–October 20, 2020), who, even in the face of terminal cancer, shared the love of Jesus with doctors, nurses, and other cancer patients, often praying with them as they awaited chemotherapy or radiation treatments.

*Rest in peace, my brother.
I will see you when I see you.*

Contents

VII *Acknowledgments*

IX *Introduction: The Voice*

1 **1**: Five Stars

21 **2**: Story Power

40 **3**: A Clear and Present Benefit

54 **4**: Attitude Check

72 **5**: Don't Golf

90 **6**: Bait

109 **7**: 90/10

127 **8**: The Biology of Rejection

147 *Epilogue: The Adventure*

Acknowledgments

The more books I write, the more I appreciate that the work of writing and selling is a team sport unto itself. I am deeply grateful to our heavenly Father for allowing me to partner with such a stud group of people.

Kris Bearss continues to amaze me with her editing skill. The "readability" of my last three books, which readers comment on regularly, is because of her. She is a master at her craft. Wayne Hastings is a veteran publisher who has a keen eye and discerning spirit for book strategy and structure. He gets what the Holy Spirit is doing and is unafraid to communicate it. And Josh Taylor has the hardest job—creating graphics and layouts for my book designs. I am notoriously difficult to work with in this regard, regularly testing Josh's patience! But he continually delivers excellent results.

Lastly, I am grateful to my heavenly Father, who relentlessly pursued me in different ways—often through people who flexed their story power so that I could become a part of His story.

Thank You, Father, for not giving up on me and for giving me a story of my own with which I can reach others and impart life through Jesus' love.

Introduction: The Voice

I was twenty-six the first time I heard the Voice.

I was in a bar. Drinking. Looking for love in all the wrong places. Just like I had many, many times before. In that regard, this night was no different from nearly every night for the previous eight years. I was just doing my thing.

Then, there it was.

I knew enough to recognize, *That isn't coming from me!* because I know what regularly tumbles around in my brain, and this was super unusual. Yet I wasn't sure where it *was* coming from.

On my own, I would never have said the things I was hearing. Nevertheless, distinct words were tumbling around in my head, in a voice I didn't recognize.

The Voice only asked two questions.

No dialogue. No back and forth. Two questions . . .

"*Are you really having fun?*"

"*Do you think this is all there is to life?*"

That was it.

I heard them once that night. And then I began to hear them regularly.

Not in the same night. Not every night. But repeatedly, on different nights while I was doing my thing. I wasn't being taunted; it felt more like I was being pursued. Still, I remember becoming annoyed at the Voice and arguing with whatever or whoever this was: "I *would* have a good time if you'd leave me alone!"

Not long after I first heard the Voice, I started a job as a recruiter at a staffing agency. I was part of a three-person team led by a guy named Brett Russell. Within a couple of months, Brett invited me to a Bible study. I had no background in church and knew practically nothing about Jesus. But there was something about Brett. Something I hadn't been around before. So I went to the study. And then I went again. And again.

Maybe three months after I started attending the studies, I gave my life to Jesus at the church Brett belonged to. That Sunday, when the pastor invited people to come forward to surrender their lives to Jesus, I stood up from the last row of the highest balcony in that building and started walking—though it was more like I was lifted and moved. I was fully aware and in control; at the same time, I was shocked at what I was doing.

Once I'd made the journey down front, I gave my life to Christ, saying, "I don't know much about this Jesus stuff. All I know is, when I hear His name, something in me comes alive. Let's get it on!"

That was my prayer of surrender. Very eloquent!

In that moment, the love of Jesus came rushing into my life. He was real. I knew His presence. Where there had been emptiness,

INTRODUCTION: THE VOICE

I was filled. Where there had been confusion, I had clarity. A passion for the Lord was birthed in me that I'd never known was available.

I was so amazed by what God was doing in me that I forgot about the Voice in the bar. Sometime later, I remembered that part of my story with joy, finally realizing: the Voice was the Holy Spirit! (As little as I knew about Jesus, I'm not sure I had even heard of the Holy Spirit before joining the Bible study.) The Spirit of God Himself had been talking to me—asking me perfectly aimed questions that awakened me to Jesus and a new life. I had indeed been pursued, urged, compelled to come to faith and be forgiven so I could enjoy love and intimacy and life in the Father, Son, and Holy Spirit.[1]

God our Father "found" me in a bar! That is awesome!

HIS PASSION FOR PEOPLE

In my walk with Jesus, I would learn of our heavenly Father's passion for reaching people.

The apostle Peter taught that the reason Jesus' return to earth (His second coming) hasn't happened yet—the reason it seems delayed—is so that more souls can be saved: "The Lord is not slow about His promise, as some count slowness, but is patient toward you, not wishing for any to perish but for all to come to

---

[1] God tells us about Himself in the Bible. He is one God—there are not multiple gods (Genesis 1:1). At the same time, He is three distinct persons—Father, Son, and Holy Spirit (Matthew 28:18–20). That the God of the Bible is three-in-one is classically referenced as "the Trinity." This can be confusing, but it is critically important. We are invited into a deep, intimate relationship with all three persons of the one true God. I wrote a chapter about Trinitarian intimacy in the first book of this series, *BE: The Way of Rest* (see chapter 4, "The Most Valuable").

repentance."[2] God the Father is leaning in, intentionally working, stirring hearts, so that everyone who *will* repent can turn from their former way of life and enter a new relationship with the One who loves them and created them.

Our heavenly Father has always had a passion for people. His main reason for creating human beings was so that we could freely enjoy fellowship and life with the Father, Son, and Holy Spirit. After creating Adam and Eve, God charged them with this instruction: "From any tree of the garden you may eat freely; but from the tree of the knowledge of good and evil you shall not eat, for in the day that you eat from it you will surely die."[3]

They each had a choice. Adam and Eve could choose to trust God and not eat from the tree of the knowledge of good and evil, remaining in perfect fellowship with their Creator. Or they could disobey and experience death and separation from their Creator.

Sadly, Adam and Eve both chose disobedience. When they committed this first sin, they broke their intimacy with God and severed themselves from the life for which they were created.

God could have easily destroyed everything, calling it quits right then and there. Instead, He chose to press on, providing an alternative plan so that Adam and Eve and all their descendants could have the opportunity to be reconciled to Him.

In Genesis 12, the Lord selected a seemingly random man, Abram (his name would later be changed by God to Abraham), to be the father of a new people-group that He was establishing.

---

[2] 2 Peter 3:9.
[3] Genesis 2:16–17.

INTRODUCTION: THE VOICE

Verses 1–3 record God's invitation to Abram not only to relocate his family to the land of Canaan but to trust Him and His plan:

> Now the LORD said to Abram, "Go forth from your country, and from your relatives and from your father's house, to the land which I will show you; and I will make you a great nation, and I will bless you, and make your name great; and so you shall be a blessing; and I will bless those who bless you, and the one who curses you I will curse. And in you all the families of the earth will be blessed."

Notice the sequence of divine blessing. First, God would bless Abram. Second, through Abram, all the families of the earth would be blessed. This was the heavenly Father's program, signaling His intense desire to reach people! He was going to establish a nation of people, the Jews, through Abram. They would live such set-apart, blessed lives that all the people of the world would marvel at their ways, be drawn to their God, and be reconnected to the One who created them in love!

God our Father was so passionate about reaching people that He created a new nation to serve as a light of blessing to the world. Unfortunately, the Jewish people repeatedly stumbled and fell, failing to follow this plan. Still, God would not be deterred. In His perfect wisdom, the Father waited for the perfect time ("the fullness of time") in the history of creation to send His ultimate "weapon"—Jesus, His Son—to pay the penalty for human sin that began with Adam and Eve. As the apostle Paul described it:

When the fullness of time came, God sent forth His Son, born of a woman, born under the Law, so that He might redeem those who were under the Law, that we might receive the adoption as sons. Because you are sons, God has sent forth the Spirit of His Son into our hearts, crying, "Abba! Father!" Therefore you are no longer a slave, but a son; and if a son, then an heir through God.[4]

Jesus came to make it possible for anyone to be forgiven of their sins and be adopted into God's family. Through Jesus' life, crucifixion, resurrection, and enthronement in heaven, the way was made for the Holy Spirit to be poured out, empowering Jesus' followers to become missionaries who would share the Good News everywhere. In one of His post-resurrection teachings, Jesus assured His disciples, "You will receive power when the Holy Spirit has come upon you; and you shall be My witnesses both in Jerusalem, and in all Judea and Samaria, and even to the remotest part of the earth."[5]

In all these things—in creation, His invitation to Abram, the gift of Jesus, the outpouring of the Holy Spirit, and the sending of His sons and daughters out into the world—our Father's passion for people is evident. As He persistently and lovingly reached you and me, so He wants to work in you and me to reach others.

BE UNIMPRESSIVE

"You are going to do *what* with *who*?"

The night before Jesus began assembling the team of men He would train to carry on His mission of saving the world, He was

---

[4] Galatians 4:4–7.
[5] Acts 1:8.

INTRODUCTION: THE VOICE

talking with His mother, Mary. Only recently had His Father in heaven told Him it was time to start His public ministry. Jesus had diligently studied the sacred texts of Judaism. He worked hard at carpentry, helping to provide for His family. All the while, He faithfully waited for His heavenly Father to say, "Go."

Jesus' baptism in the Jordan River by His cousin John the Baptist signaled the beginning of that earthly ministry. When the Holy Spirit descended on Jesus, the Father's voice was heard from above, saying: "You are My beloved Son, in You I am well-pleased."[6] Led afterward by the Spirit into the wilderness, Jesus faithfully fasted forty days and then overcame the guile and temptations of Satan.[7] After this, Jesus began preaching, healing the sick, and freeing those who were demon-possessed.

The first time He preached in His hometown of Nazareth, His audience was "filled with rage," and they ran Him out of town to throw Him off a cliff.[8] I don't know how well your first time of sharing the gospel went, but Jesus' experience takes a lot of pressure off those of us who worry about our hearers liking us.

Following these events, the time came for Him to choose and commission His first disciples. Under the strategic direction of His Father, and through the guidance of the Holy Spirit, Jesus identified the first four men on His team. In excitement, He shared the news with Mary.

She remembered the incredible manner of Jesus' birth. She knew her son was divinely purposed. But while she had witnessed

---

[6] Mark 1:11.
[7] Luke 4:1–13.
[8] Luke 4:14–30.

many great works of His already, she questioned His discernment in choosing His first disciples.

If you were going to establish a global business empire, surely you would select from the finest business schools in the world. If you were building a dominant military, surely you would recruit the sharpest men and women from the top military academies. Jesus' first four recruits, however, were . . . fishermen. Guys who got up every day and did nothing but cast nets into water, pull in those nets, empty the nets of fish, and repeat—again and again and again.

The next day in Capernaum, a city on the Sea of Galilee where Jesus headquartered most of His ministry, He saw the four men—Peter, James, John, and Andrew—washing their nets, and He asked to come aboard one of Peter's boats. After teaching a crowd who had gathered on the shore, Jesus directed Peter to deeper water. There, Peter caught such a great haul of fish that his partners in the other boats had to come help him pull in the nets.

The men were amazed. Jesus used this as both symbol and segue to say to them, "Follow Me, and I will make you become fishers of men."[9]

These fishermen had no idea of the breadth and depth of Jesus' invitation. All they knew was that they had to GO. They had to follow. "When they had brought their boats to land, they left everything and followed Him."[10]

Judging by what she could see with her eyes, Mary was right to be concerned. But Jesus could see what Mary did not. God the

---

[9] Mark 1:17.
[10] Luke 5:11.

Father had chosen these men for this work. Our Father knew what He was doing then, and He knows what He is doing now, with us.

You must know this: God has a long history of using very unimpressive people to do very impressive things. Abram (a nomad), Moses (an adoptee), Rahab (a prostitute), Gideon (an illegitimate son), Hannah (a woman of faith who dealt with infertility), Saul (a member of the tribe of Benjamin, the smallest of Israel's tribes), Amos (a shepherd), Stephen (a layman), Timothy (a boy), and many others had very unimpressive beginnings. Jesus' parents, Joseph and Mary, had exceedingly ordinary resumés. Even Jesus Himself was not impressive to look at! Notice the prophet Isaiah's description of the Savior: "He has no stately form or majesty that we should look upon Him, nor appearance that we should be attracted to Him."[11] If you are a Christian, your Father in heaven has chosen you to help carry on the mission of Jesus, advancing His kingdom by sharing the good news of salvation with those who don't yet believe. *Yes, He has chosen you!* You've been recruited to join God's team of unimpressive missionaries.

WE ARE SENT

In *BE: The Way of Rest*, I talked about organics. *Organics* describes the relationship between a person's beliefs, practices, and results. We looked at Psalm 23:1 and discovered how our practices and results are transformed when we believe both that the Lord is our Shepherd and that we are simply sheep. In John 15:5, we saw how

---

[11] Isaiah 53:2.

believing that Jesus is our Vine and we His branches naturally leads to abiding in Him and a life that produces much fruit.

Effective GO-ing begins with what we believe. We must believe that God our Father is sending us. We must believe the significance of the gospel message. We must believe the importance of sharing it. As we believe these things, our practices will naturally become those of missionaries who have been sent. For that is who we are. As our practices align with our beliefs, we will begin to see the results—the great catch of fish—that Jesus wants us to experience.

At the end of our Lord's time on earth, He left His disciples with one final command: to carry on His mission to reach others with the gospel. Both Matthew and Mark record what is called the Great Commission.

> Jesus came up and spoke to them, saying, "All authority has been given to Me in heaven and on earth. Go therefore and make disciples of all the nations, baptizing them in the name of the Father and the Son and the Holy Spirit, teaching them to observe all that I commanded you; and lo, I am with you always, even to the end of the age." (Matthew 28:18–20)

> He said to them, "Go into all the world and preach the gospel to all creation. He who has believed and has been baptized shall be saved; but he who has disbelieved shall be condemned." (Mark 16:15–16)

Jesus commanded His team of unimpressive trainees to "Go . . . and make disciples." The Greek word for "go" is in the imperative voice, meaning this is a command, not a suggestion. Jesus our Lord was commissioning His followers to go and keep reaching people for Him. This is the calling that makes every Christian a missionary.

Whoever you think of when you think of a missionary, you need to include yourself! Whatever vision you have of a missionary's life, your life is *that* life! Yes, missionaries go to foreign countries. Yes, missionaries help the poor and the widowed and the addicted and those in prison. Missionaries also . . . bake cookies for neighbors, watch friends' houses, host community parties, lead secular businesses, and do a lot of other works in order to faithfully fulfill their commission from Jesus.

Every missionary's heart is to share the gospel. While we love feeding the homeless, building homes for the needy, and binding up the broken, our great passion must be to share the love and life of Jesus in a way that the ones we touch will repent, convert to the one true God who loves them, and be saved. We want all people to enter into a healthy, growing relationship with the Father, Son, and Holy Spirit.

Although our heavenly Father has certainly gifted some people as missionaries, He wants to work through every one of us to reach others. Like the haul of fish that Jesus directed Peter to in Luke 5, our Father has a great haul of souls He wants His sons and daughters to catch. My friend Clint loves catching. Recently he said to me, "There's a big difference between fishing and catching!" As missionaries for the Lord, as His fishers of men (and women), let us become experts at catching those to whom our Father sends us.

Learning to share the gospel is not something you have to do on your own, or through sheer force of the will. This is something Jesus taught every one of His followers to do. He invited His first, unimpressive four to the work, saying, "*I will make you become fishers of men.*"[12] You are not responsible for training yourself to effectively share the gospel or to overcome the issues that keep you from sharing. You're responsible for letting Jesus develop you into a fisher of people.

The only prerequisite is to allow Christ, through the Holy Spirit, to do what He wants to do in you. Instead of trying to prove to the world that you are somehow impressive, you can go forth as one who has been commissioned by Jesus Himself. Rather than wallowing in how unimpressive you are (as many Christians do), you can go in the assurance of the One who has sent you.

Ideally, a veteran "fisherman" would be available to show you how to share the gospel message. Somebody who has spent years honing their ability to tell others about Jesus would bring you with them. This is the primary way Jesus trained His disciples: by modeling it for them. Then He sent them out in pairs of two to do what they had watched Him do.

Sadly, we do not have as many lifelong fishermen as we have novices who need to be trained. Therefore, we supplement those missing role models with books and other useful tools.

I wrote *BE: The Way of Rest* to electrify your relationship with Jesus so that when you GO, you can do so in the overflow of what the Spirit is already doing in your life. We certainly don't want

---

[12] Mark 1:17.

our presentation of the gospel to sound like a spiel for timeshares! Jesus calls us to an authentic, vibrant, personal, heartfelt communication of the Good News. That was His way, and it should be ours as His disciples.

THE MOST IMPORTANT MESSAGE

A long time ago, I read a quote somewhere that I've never been able to find again but that I've never forgotten either. It was one of those lines that so penetrates you, you only have to encounter it once. The quote went something like this: "Every time you preach, do so as if the eternity of men's souls hangs in the balance."

I remember reading and then rereading those words, captivated by their intensity. Whoever wrote this (please contact me if you know the source) wanted to stir up those who preach to remember what is at stake when we preach.

I think all Christians need the same sober statement today with respect to sharing the gospel. Every day you live, in every interaction you have with others, live and interact as if their souls hang in the balance eternally.

The gospel is the single-most important message in the history of humanity. And, it always will be. No other statement or body of information compares. There is nothing that has been learned or will be learned that is more critical to our existence than the gospel detailing the life, death, burial, resurrection, ascension, and enthronement of the Son of God. For what is greater than our eternal destiny? Not curing cancer. Not ending poverty. Not stopping pollution.

Mark 1:14–15 records Jesus' first public sermon. He is about to speak the first words of His public ministry to begin fulfilling His Father's plan. What would He say? "The time is fulfilled, and the kingdom of God is at hand; repent and believe in the gospel."

The gospel is so critical to life that it is the content of the Son of God's first sermon.

It is consequential because the gospel is the dividing line between heaven and hell. Jesus told a powerful story in Luke 16:19–31 about an unnamed rich man and a poor man named Lazarus. Both die. The poor man is carried away by angels to Abraham's bosom.[13] The rich man ends up in Hades, tormented.[14] Seeing Abraham across a great chasm, the rich man cries out, begging the patriarch to send Lazarus to him "so that he may dip the tip of his finger in water and cool off my tongue, for I am in agony in this flame" (verse 24). Abraham cannot do this because a chasm stands between them that no one can cross. So the tormented rich man begs Abraham to send Lazarus to his family "in order that he may warn them, so that they will not also come to this place of torment" (verse 28). The rich man desperately wants someone, anyone, to be sent to his family to share the gospel! We can assume that, during his life, the rich man believed that information leading to wealth and power was most important. In his death, he learned he had bought into a lie. In fact, the gospel is most important.

What is at stake in the gospel is not complicated. Those who receive its message, surrendering to Jesus, will spend eternity with

---

[13] "Abraham's bosom" is a figure of speech representing the blessing of life that is to come for the one who perseveres in Christ.

[14] While Hades can refer to the generic, intermediate location of the dead (both believing and unbelieving), here it refers to the portion of Hades reserved for those who die apart from Christ.

Him in the new heaven and earth. Those who reject the gospel are rejecting Jesus and will spend eternity separated from their Creator in the lake of fire, hell. What information could possibly be more important than the gospel?

I was sharing Jesus with a man one time who redirected our conversation to a hot-button political issue. After telling me where he stood and that he was not going to change, he pressed me on what I thought. I said, "It seems like you've spent a lot of time thinking about this issue. I hope you'll spend even more time thinking about what will happen to you when you die. You will be dead a lot longer than you live."

Besides eternal life, the gospel is consequential because it leads to ABUNDANT LIFE today! It's very unfortunate that so many people believe in Jesus solely as a means to eternal life; meanwhile they miss out on the abundant life He offers. Can you fathom the difference Jesus has made in the quality of your life today? Can you imagine what state you would be in if He had not rescued you?

The gospel is transformational. It is joy! It is electricity and energy! It is living hope! There is so much LIFE packed into its message, and Jesus wants to impart every bit of it to anyone who will follow Him.

We have furniture sellers who talk really loudly in their commercials about the ENORMOUS(!) sales on their merchandise. Their volume leaves little doubt about what they're offering. Other advertisers feature their products or services in bright lights on huge billboards to draw attention and communicate their message.

Jesus could not have been clearer about the life that is available only through the gospel:

- "Everyone who drinks of this water will thirst again; but whoever drinks of the water that I will give him shall never thirst; but the water that I will give him will become in him a well of water springing up to eternal life."[15]
- "You search the Scriptures because you think that in them you have eternal life; it is these that testify about Me; and you are unwilling to come to Me so that you may have life."[16]
- "The thief comes only to steal and kill and destroy; I came that they may have life, and have it abundantly."[17]

The apostle Paul tasted the excelling quality of gospel life when he surrendered to Jesus. In Philippians 3:2–6, Paul listed some of his top worldly accomplishments. These achievements had brought him status and power before his conversion. Then he met Jesus and everything changed. In verses 7–8, Paul explained, "But whatever things were gain to me, those things I have counted as loss for the sake of Christ. More than that, I count all things to be loss in view of the surpassing value of knowing Christ Jesus my Lord."

The apostle experienced the "surpassing value" of gospel life in Christ and immediately regarded all his other life experiences as

---

[15] John 4:13–14.
[16] John 5:39–40.
[17] John 10:10.

loss! So it's no wonder that in Romans he enthusiastically affirmed: "He who believes in Him will not be disappointed" (9:33, referring to the prophet's message in Isaiah 28:16) and "Just as it is written, 'How beautiful are the feet of those who bring good news of good things!'" (10:15, quoting Isaiah 52:7).

GO-TIME!

Sports leagues operate according to seasons. First there's preseason, then the regular season, which leads to the playoffs and culminates in the championship. Businesses operate according to seasons as well, often dividing their calendar year into quarters: Q1, Q2, Q3, Q4. Different quarters trigger different strategic focuses. King Solomon famously summed up this aspect of life in Ecclesiastes 3:1: "There is an appointed time [season] for everything. And there is a time for every event under heaven."

Brothers and sisters, your season of stepping into your calling as a kingdom missionary has begun. Now is GO-time!

Of course you have fears and doubts. This book talks about those, offering ways of overcoming them and allowing the Holy Spirit to speak into them.

Of course you need clarity. Keep reading—it's coming.

Of course you want easy-to-use techniques that don't feel forced. We will get to them.

The Holy Spirit wants to ignite an urgency in you to reach people with the Good News. In my mind, I see a scenario in which our Father has created a divine appointment for you to share Jesus with someone. We will pause the scene just as you are about to speak and, in this book, we will break down the elements and dynamics of this opportunity: What are the Father, Son, and Holy Spirit doing? How are your fears and anxieties? What could you say? Then I want to press Play and talk through the kinds of reactions you can expect.

My ambitious goal for you in the Lord is that you BE alive in Christ, GO to effectively share Jesus with others, and then MAKE disciples of those who say yes to Him. Those disciples will then BE, GO, and MAKE within their generations. By the grace of our Father, co-laboring with the Holy Spirit in the name of Jesus, we will succeed in fulfilling the mission of the kingdom of heaven!

You—yes, you—are a part of the Creator's plan to rescue people from condemnation and to save them from their sins so they can know Jesus, His love, His life, His eternal comfort.

Let's be unimpressive.

Let's be wise.

Let's be clear.

Let's be faithful.

Let's be unafraid.

LET'S GO!

1 Five Stars

"You have to try Lupe Tortilla!" I excitedly share with anyone who visits Houston. For Tex-Mex food in this city, you cannot beat Lupe. The queso is fantastic. The seasoning in the fajita beef is mouthwatering, and their homemade tortillas are enormous!

Thanks to Houston's ethnic diversity, the city has excellent restaurants in a wide variety of cuisines. But how would anyone know where to get really good BBQ, Ethiopian food, or Indian food? Where do you go to get the best burger or pizza? The best way I've found to avoid a bad restaurant experience is to read the recommendations of previous customers. The Internet is loaded with websites dedicated to recommendations and reviews of restaurants as well as just about any product or service a person could ever need.

Nearly every one of us has stories to tell of great experiences we've had because we trusted someone's recommendation. And inevitably, we feel grateful because those are experiences we would never have had—never would've heard of—apart from someone's willingness to speak up.

Trusted recommendations carry great power and influence.

SCORING JESUS

When was the last time *you* recommended a book, movie, or restaurant to someone? When you made the recommendation, did you initiate the conversation or did you offer your suggestion in response to something within the conversation?

On a scale of 1 to 5, what was the level of experience that prompted you to make the recommendation? Was it a 5? Maybe a 4?

Most of us wouldn't recommend something that rated less than a 3.5 on our personal scale. If a restaurant, book, or movie is around a 4, we would probably happily recommend it. If the restaurant, book, or movie rates a 4.5 or a 5, we often initiate the recommendation: "You have to try _____!"

Marketing professionals and others who specialize in consumer response have often said, "Word of mouth is the best advertising." This holds just as true in our social media–driven world as it did in ancient times. Think of it. In the garden of Eden, Adam ate the apple at Eve's recommendation and Eve ate upon hearing the serpent's "recommendation."

Testimonials have always been persuasive. According to researchers, when it comes to people's purchasing decisions, "there is strong evidence . . . that consumers rely on customer [that's you!] recommendations far more than advertising."[1]

---

[1] Key Pousttchi and Dietmar Wiedemann, *Handbook of Research on Mobile Marketing Management* (New York: Business Science Reference, 2010), 402.

Understanding the enormous persuasive power of recommendation, why do we as devoted followers of Jesus so often hesitate to recommend Him? If you were to rate your experience with Jesus on a scale of 1 to 5, what would be your score?

Maybe that's the issue. Maybe Jesus just isn't that much of a factor in your daily quality of life. Maybe He scores in the 2.5 range for you. When was the last time you recommended a restaurant that you thought was a 2.5 out of 5?

Scoring Jesus as a 2 to 3 is common among Christians who live in what I call "the tortured middle," that flavorless, desolate place between renouncing Jesus as Lord and abiding in Him. No one wants to live in the tortured middle, let alone recommend that others join you there. Everybody wants the five-star experience!

Of the variety of reasons we get trapped in the middle, most often it's because we lack clarity and confidence regarding what it means to follow Jesus. Developing intimacy with God the Father, Jesus the Son, and the Holy Spirit can be confusing. Warring against our enemies—sin, the world, and Satan—is difficult and uncomfortable. And understanding how to trust in our Father's faithfulness for daily living doesn't always come easily.

The first book in this series, *BE*, offers a recipe for following Jesus that can liberate you from the tortured middle and free you to fully experience life with Him. Once you're dwelling in a five-star existence, you're ready to GO, sharing the love of Jesus with others. If you aren't there yet in your faith, I'd encourage you to take some time and read *BE: The Way of Rest*. For now, sit in prayer and ask our Father to show you what He wants to do in you so that you can experience the five-star life Jesus offers.

FIVE-STAR WATER

The pattern of biblical evangelism goes like this: an individual who is on fire for Jesus, experiencing the incredible miracle of living in Him daily, goes forth to tell others about the five-star life they can have in deep relationship with Jesus. For those who say yes to Jesus, we co-labor with the Holy Spirit to train them, making them into mature, wise disciples who then go and share with others.

Throughout this book we will look at different evangelism stories (within the Bible and elsewhere) to learn what we can from them. We will observe a variety of approaches that Christians use to effectively communicate the gospel. We will also learn that not every effort succeeds, which helps to alleviate the pressure many of us put on ourselves. Seeing people who are really good at sharing the gospel strike out sometimes helps me relax when it's my turn to GO.

Our first story, from John 4, recounts a time when Jesus grew thirsty while traveling through Samaria, a region located between Jerusalem to the south and Galilee to the north. Finding the local water well in the Samarian city of Sychar, Jesus sits there to rest. A woman "just so happens" to approach. He asks her for a drink. The woman is confused. You can almost see her tilting her head with eyes narrowed, trying to process what's going on. This conversation has already violated cultural practices of the day, for Jews did not interact with Samaritans.

The woman voices her confusion: "How is it that You, being a Jew, ask me for a drink since I am a Samaritan woman?" (verse 9).

Jesus brushes past the social issue to get at the heart of the matter: the quality of the water. He replies, "If you knew the gift of God, and who it is who says to you, 'Give Me a drink,' you would have asked Him, and He would have given you living water" (verse 10).

The woman locks in on the phrase "living water." She doesn't understand what that is or how Jesus is going to be able to draw out living water from the well.

Jesus clarifies, probably gesturing at the actual water in the well, "Everyone who drinks of this [natural] water will thirst again; but whoever drinks of the water that I will give him shall never thirst; but the water that I will give him will become in him a well of water springing up to eternal life" (verses 13–14).

Jesus just recommended His water to the woman, telling her, "That natural water there is one-star water; My supernatural water is five-star. Well water can satisfy you physically. The water I offer will give you eternal life!"

If you really want great water, get it from Jesus!

Notice, too, that Jesus doesn't only say, "My water is better than yours." He promises the woman she will experience the specific benefit of eternal life if she trusts His recommendation and drinks His water. Similarly, when you recommend a restaurant, don't you give specific reasons why? I'm not telling you to try Lupe Tortilla just because it's a place to eat in Houston. I'm telling you go to Lupe Tortilla because you will love their queso, fajita meat, and tortillas!

Jesus knew the power of recommendation. He knew the power of contrasting His five-star water with other water. "If you are truly thirsty, you need My water. It's the best water on the planet! Mine will give you eternal life."

For Jesus, a five-star life was easy to talk about and recommend because He lived it! He knew how much better it was than the alternative.

Five-star life was the experience of Peter the apostle as well. In 1 Peter 2, he reminded his disciples of God's incredible nature and His work in their lives. The Almighty would be the one to organically propel their GO: "You are a chosen race, a royal priesthood, a holy nation, a people for God's own possession, so that you may proclaim the excellencies of Him who has called you out of darkness into His marvelous light" (verse 9).

Peter marveled at God's work. Can you imagine having a "royal priesthood" bestowed on you? Christ has changed your life! He has changed your title, your identity. And these five-star realities compel us to go forth as missionaries to "proclaim [His] excellencies." Peter doesn't say we should go out and share what is *meh*, average, or pretty good. What we have to share is exquisite! Brilliant! Exceptional! Superb! Tremendous!

Let us not shrink back as if Jesus' life and work in and through us is anything less than five stars. Let us so fully soak in the excellencies of what He has done, is doing, and will do that we excitedly GO and share from our overflow, joyfully announcing to others, "YOU NEED THE GIFT I'VE BEEN GIVEN! YOU'RE GOING TO WANT THE EXPERIENCE I'VE HAD!"

SMILE

"Smile and dial" is a standard phrase in telesales. New salespeople are continually told that prospective customers can "hear your smile" through the phone, and three psychologists at the University of Portsmouth in the United Kingdom proved it! They studied the effects of smiling on one's tone of voice and whether listeners could tell the difference when they couldn't see the person talking. The study showed not only that "listeners can discriminate different smile types" but that listeners can "discern *whether* a person is smiling."[2] People *can* hear your smile!

The first public sermon from Jesus is recorded in Mark 1:15–16. Jesus declared, "The time is fulfilled, and the kingdom of God is at hand; repent and believe in the gospel." His sermon invited people to accept His gospel. The word "gospel" in the Greek means "good news." The Greek term originates from the same word in Hebrew. In those days, when Israel won a war, runners would spread the "good news" of victory throughout the land.

As you imagine the faces of those runners as they spread the "gospel," what do you see? As you imagine Jesus' face during His first public sermon, what do you see? Jesus called His message "good news"! Do you think He was sad? Do you think He was emotionless? Do you think He sounded like a Shakespearean actor? No! It is good news! The best of news!

The smile we have from our relationship with Jesus is not a fake, pasted-on grin. You didn't have to manufacture your enthusiasm for the five-star restaurant you went to. The person you were talking to could see, hear, and feel your excitement! I'm not asking you to fake anything in your recommendation of Christ either. That doesn't help you overcome your fear of evangelism, and it certainly

---

[2] Amy Drahota, Alan Costall, and Vasudevi Reddy, "The Vocal Communication of Different Kinds of Smile," *Speech Communication*, vol. 50, April 2008, emphasis added, https://www.sciencedirect.com/science/article/abs/pii/S0167639307001732/.

doesn't draw in your listeners. I'm asking you to sit with Jesus and evaluate how GOOD your life is *because* of Him. Meditate on His unwavering faithfulness to you. Let these thoughts and memories sink in. Do you feel the emotion? Recalling what Jesus has done in our lives organically produces enthusiasm and joy!

Remember, you are going to be sharing the Good News. Many times, the first person you need to share that good news with is yourself!

I HAVE A PERSON!

One of my best friends, Mike Sellars, owned an investigative services agency. If you needed a private investigator, you needed Mike.

Not long ago, before Mike passed away, I was talking with a lady who needed help like his in another state. She was frustrated because she didn't know any private investigators or how to find one.

"I have a guy!" I told her. And I excitedly recommended Mike.

How many times have you said, "I have a person!"? It could be an insurance person, a lawyer, a doctor, a veterinarian, a counselor, or some other somebody. You have people. And you love recommending them!

In Jesus, you have the ultimate person.

Stress? I have the man!

Career decision? I have the man!

Financial problems? I have the man!

Marriage problems? I have the man!

Despair? Emptiness? I have the man!

Organizational issues? I have the man!

As we go to share, we go to share Jesus. We're not sharing church, denomination, or religion. We're sharing the truth that the Son of God is alive and well, knocking on the door of peoples' lives so that He can come in and do what He does.

In Mark 7, Jesus was back in the region of the Sea of Galilee, the area where He conducted most of His early ministry. The Decapolis, a cluster of ten cities, was to the northeast. One day while in the Decapolis, Jesus encountered a man who was deaf and had trouble speaking. Jesus and the man left the crowd for a one-on-one meeting. The Son of God put His fingers in the man's ears and, after spitting, touched the man's tongue with some of His saliva. Mark 7:34 tells us that Jesus then commanded the man's ears, "Be opened!"—and the one who had been deaf was instantly healed. Jesus' reputation spread like wildfire. "They were utterly astonished, saying, 'He has done all things well; He makes even the deaf to hear and the mute to speak'" (verse 37).

The church didn't heal this guy. A denomination didn't restore his hearing. Religion didn't cure his speech. Jesus did. The man had a one-on-one encounter with a person, Jesus Christ.

In your own story, you weren't saved by the church, a denomination, or religion either. You encountered Jesus! As a Christian, you live in relationship with Jesus, the person. His presence in your life affects you.

My friend Lynn is sixty-five years old. When Lynn was five, her mom turned on the TV one day and said, "You can watch TV while I make a quick run to the store." Lynn remembers someone on a show that day saying, "Jesus is here with you"—a comforting reminder for a little girl at home alone for a few minutes.

Those words stayed with her. When Lynn was fifteen, three of her girlfriends took her to a Youth for Christ rally where she heard about Jesus again. Six weeks later, at a Campus Life event, she began wrestling with the question "How do you know Jesus is there?" That night, in her room and on her knees, Lynn met Jesus and surrendered her life to Him. She says, "The next day in school I had an unbelievable desire to love people!"

Jesus continues to work in lives today. He does not disappoint. And He will not fail. Find confidence in *Who* you are sharing more than *what* you are sharing. Never forget—you have the person!

THE AMERICAN NIGHTMARE

Years ago I was on a mission trip in Nicaragua. One of the women on our team was working with some young children. Reading out of the book of Revelation, she began to describe a place where the streets were lined with gold, the sky was filled with brilliant light, and the people did not cry. She asked the kids, "Where am I describing?"

One girl shouted, "America!"

Americans are certainly accomplished at looking like we have it all together. Social media gives us lots of opportunities to open the doors of our lives so that others can see the good stuff.

Are we really as happy and peace-filled as our posts declare? If we have it all together, do we need the gospel? If our nice houses and pretty smiles are the result of internal stability and peace, then why would we need Jesus?

We need Him because, according to statistics, the land of opportunity is a poor cover for a nation in pain. Consider the following:

- Nearly 620,000 abortions were performed in 2018.[3]
- Almost 13 percent of Americans are alcoholics.[4]
- More than 130 Americans died every day from opioid overdose in 2017.[5]
- Vaping/e-cigarette use grew 900 percent between 2011 and 2015.[6]
- Diabetes is projected to affect nearly 55 million Americans by 2030—a 54 percent increase from the number of cases in 2015.[7]
- The US obesity rate was at an all-time high of 42.4 percent in 2018.[8]
- In 2018, more than 17.7 million surgical and minimally invasive cosmetic procedures were performed in the United States.[9]

---

[3] "Data and Statistics," Centers for Disease Control and Prevention, accessed January 7, 2021, https://www.cdc.gov/reproductivehealth/data_stats/index.htm/.

[4] Bridget F. Grant, S. Patricia Chou, Tulshi D. Saha, "Prevalence of 12-Month Alcohol Use, High-Risk Drinking, and *DSM-IV* Alcohol Use Disorder in the United States, 2001–2002 to 2012–2013," JAMA Network, September 2017, https://jamanetwork.com/journals/jamapsychiatry/fullarticle/2647079/.

[5] "Data Brief 329. Drug Overdose Deaths in the United States, 1999–2017," accessed January 7, 2021, https://www.cdc.gov/nchs/data/databriefs/db329_tables-508.pdf#page=4/.

[6] "E-Cigarette Use Among Youth and Young Adults: A Report of the Surgeon General," U.S. Department of Health and Human Services, 2016, https://e-cigarettes.surgeongeneral.gov/documents/2016_SGR_Full_Report_non-508.pdf.

[7] William R. Rowley, Clement Bezoid, Yasemin Arikan, Erin Byrne, and Shannon Krohe, "Diabetes 2030: Insights from Yesterday, Today, and Future Trends," *Population Health Management*, February 1, 2017, https://www.ncbi.nlm.nih.gov/pmc/articles/PMC5278808/.

[8] "Adult Obesity Facts," Centers for Disease Control and Prevention, accessed January 7, 2021, https://www.cdc.gov/obesity/data/adult.html/.

[9] "2018 National Plastic Surgery Statistics," American Society of Plastic Surgeons, https://www.plasticsurgery.org/documents/News/Statistics/2018/plastic-surgery-statistics-report-2018.pdf/.

- In 2019, an estimated 51.5 million adults aged eighteen or older were diagnosed with some form of mental illness.[10]
- An estimated 18.1 percent of adults (40 million) are affected by anxiety disorders every year.[11]
- More than 48,000 Americans committed suicide in 2018. Suicide is the second-leading cause of death among individuals between the ages of 10 and 34.[12]
- Nearly half of Americans report sometimes or always feeling alone or left out.[13]
- Household debt rose to a difficult-to-fathom $14.35 trillion in 2020,[14] while student-loan debt rose to $1.55 trillion in the third quarter of 2020.[15]
- An estimated 40 to 50 percent of first-time marriages end in divorce.[16]
- In 2014 (the most current stats available), pornography

---

[10] Mental Health Information: Statistics: Mental Illness, National Institute of Mental Health, accessed January 7, 2021, https://www.nimh.nih.gov/health/statistics/mental-illness.shtml.

[11] "Did You Know?" Facts & Statistics, Anxiety and Depression Association of America, accessed January 14, 2021, https://adaa.org/about-adaa/press-room/facts-statistics/.

[12] Mental Health Information: Suicide, National Institute of Mental Health, accessed January 8, 2021, https://www.nimh.nih.gov/health/statistics/suicide.shtml.

[13] Ellie Polack, "New Cigna Study Reveals Loneliness at Epidemic Levels in America," Cigna, *Newsroom*, May 1, 2018, https://www.cigna.com/newsroom/news-releases/2018/new-cigna-study-reveals-loneliness-at-epidemic-levels-in-america/.

[14] "Household Debt and Credit," Center for Microeconomic Data, Federal Reserve Bank of New York, accessed January 9, 2021, https://www.newyorkfed.org/microeconomics/hhdc/background.html.

[15] "Quarterly Report on Household Debt and Credit: 2020: Q3," Federal Reserve Bank of New York, Center for Microeconomic Data, November 2020, https://www.newyorkfed.org/medialibrary/interactives/householdcredit/data/pdf/HHDC_2020Q3.pdf.

[16] "Marriage and Divorce," adapted from the *Encyclopedia of Psychology*, American Psychological Association, accessed January 9, 2021, https://www.apa.org/topics/divorce/.

was a $10 to $12 billion industry in the United States, and a $97 billion industry globally.[17] Those numbers have undoubtedly exploded since then.
- By 2019, "the number of [online] photos and videos of children being sexually abused" had risen to more than 45 million. In 1998 there were approximately 3,000 photos and videos online.[18]

Maybe we need to rename the American Dream the American Nightmare. It is certainly not producing a five-star life.

Your family, friends, and neighbors *need* Jesus. I don't care how "together" they seem or how beautiful their families are on social media, every single person you know is dealing with the brokenness of this world. I've spent so much time with people whose social media posts would provoke envy for anybody, only to discover their behind-closed-doors life is falling apart.

In Mark 2, Jesus came across a tax collector named Levi. Jesus said to him, "'Follow Me!' And he got up and followed Him" (verse 14). I wish winning people to the Lord was that easy for me!

Immediately after this exchange, Jesus went to Levi's house, where they were joined by others who were considered the scourge of society. The religious leaders of the day, the scribes and Pharisees, were shocked. "Why is He eating and drinking with tax collectors and sinners?" Jesus replied, "It is not those who are

---

[17] "Things Are Looking Up in America's Porn Industry," NBC News, January 20, 2015, https://www.nbcnews.com/business/business-news/things-are-looking-americas-porn-industry-n289431/.

[18] Michael H. Keller and Gabriel J. X. Dance, "The Internet Is Overrun with Images of Child Sexual Abuse. What Went Wrong?" *New York Times,* September 20, 2019, https://www.nytimes.com/interactive/2019/09/28/us/child-sex-abuse.html.

healthy who need a physician, but those who are sick; I did not come to call the righteous, but sinners" (verses 16–17).

Americans are sick. People are sick. Not everyone wants to admit their sickness (a prerequisite for successful evangelism); nevertheless, American culture naturally produces great kingdom candidates. The American Dream doesn't work. You don't need to take a foreign mission trip to be surrounded by people who need Jesus. There are plenty of people in the places you normally go who are waiting for someone to share Jesus with them.

In fact (and this is cool), as you pursue your heavenly Father's will in everyday life, He will place people in your path who you can uniquely reach! This is a strategic move on His part for you to reach that person who might otherwise never go to church.

We've already seen in John 4 how Jesus was in the right place at the right time to minister to a woman at a well. After saying yes to Jesus' living water, she went back to her village and told her family and friends everything that had just happened. Scripture says, "From that city many of the Samaritans believed in Him because of the word of the woman who testified, 'He told me all the things that I have done'" (verse 39).

The woman didn't have to go looking for people to evangelize. She went to her friends and family. She was uniquely positioned to reach those people in a way that others couldn't.

HIT RATE

Hitting a Major League baseball is said to be the hardest thing to do in all of sports. A pitcher stands 60 feet, 6 inches from home plate, hurling a ball up to 100 miles per hour with incredible precision and control—even making the ball spin in different directions to affect its trajectory.

At Major League speed, the ball takes as little as 400 milliseconds to cross the plate. Hitters need about 175 milliseconds to react and 150 milliseconds to swing the bat, leaving only 75 milliseconds to determine where the pitch is going![19] So it's no surprise that in 2020, the batting average in professional baseball was .245.[20]

The best baseball players in the world succeed in getting a hit only 25 percent of the time! This sets every hitter's expectation. If you expect 50 percent success as a hitter, you're going to be tremendously disappointed.

Jesus wasn't 100 percent successful in His own evangelistic efforts either. In fact, many more people walked away from Him than became His followers. We see this clearly in John 6. Jesus had just finished feeding 5,000 people. (Bible scholars estimate the number was closer to 12,000 once women and children are factored in.) Afterward, the crowd followed Jesus to the other side of the Sea of Galilee.

The next day, Jesus proclaimed to them, "Truly, truly, I say to you, you seek Me, not because you saw signs, but because you ate of the loaves and were filled" (verse 26). Most of the people followed Him not because they believed He was the Son of God but because He satisfied their bellies. As He continued explaining

---

[19] David Coburn, "Baseball Physics: Anatomy of a Home Run," December 18, 2009, *Popular Mechanics*, https://www.popularmechanics.com/adventure/sports/a4569/4216783/.

[20] "Major League Baseball Batting Year-by-Year Averages," Baseball Reference, accessed January 9, 2021, https://www.baseball-reference.com/leagues/MLB/bat.shtml/.

what following Him truly means, individuals and families within the crowd began walking away. "As a result of [His teaching] many of His disciples withdrew and were not walking with Him anymore" (verse 66).

While Jesus wanted to be 100 percent successful in reaching souls for salvation, He knew that was not going to happen. The human heart is stubborn; most people will not open their ears to hear the truth. It makes sense, then, that when Jesus trained His disciples in evangelism, He properly calibrated their expectations of success.

His parable of the soils is found in Matthew 13, Mark 4, and Luke 8.[21] Jesus likened evangelism to a farmer going out to sow seed in a field. The seed, which is the gospel, falls on four different types of soil. In the first soil, the devil comes and steals the word of God so that the individual will not believe and be saved. In the second soil, the person responds with joy but, because there is no firm root, he or she easily falls away. The third soil bears no fruit to maturity because the person's belief is choked out by the worries of the world.

The prospects seem grim! This is not going well at all.

Thankfully, Jesus says of the fourth soil, "These are the ones who have heard the word in an honest and good heart, and hold it fast, and bear fruit with perseverance" (Luke 8:15).

One out of four.

Whether Jesus meant that we will see success only about 25 percent of the time or He was simply describing four typical reactions,

---

[21] Specifically, Matthew 13:1–23; Mark 4:1–20; and Luke 8:4–15.

He certainly communicated this challenge of evangelism.

Another challenge for us in our humanness is that we aren't inclined toward efforts where we can't easily succeed. We give up exercise because we don't see instant results. We hate long projects because they are . . . long. We don't naturally engage in pursuits where we may fail 75 percent of the time. In evangelism, we need the mentality of a Major League batter: we must absolutely approach the plate every time with a desire to get a hit. We must share the gospel each time, hoping the person will say yes to Jesus. However, we also can't let ourselves be surprised when we strike out. And we do not beat up ourselves when we don't get a hit.

Sharing the gospel is not easy. According to Jesus, people's hearts are hard. And some are harder than others. Nevertheless, we press on.

A GOOD STARTING PLACE

In the introduction, I mentioned a scenario where Father God creates an opportunity for you to share Jesus with someone, but we hit Pause just before you speak.

Now let me ask you this. After reading this chapter, do you believe you truly have something to offer the person you're about to speak to? Do you believe that because of Jesus your "water" is better—incomparably more refreshing, more thirst-quenching, more pure—than what they've ever had? Do you believe that, because of Jesus, you have a five-star life?

For years I've heard how incredible Killen's Barbecue is. The restaurant opened in Pearland, Texas, thirty minutes south of Houston, in 2013. Their "Q" is so good that they're well known for their daily lines out the door. In early 2020, I finally went. I met a friend there who had been there many times and told me I had to try it. We arrived a few minutes before opening so we wouldn't have to wait. I ordered two meats—turkey and brisket—with two sides, corn and beans. While the corn, beans, and turkey were decent, the brisket was melt-in-your-mouth fantastic. It was easy to see why this place was so highly recommended. (I was also told they have incredible chocolate cake, though I was very disappointed that they were sold out of it on the day I was there. I'm not a "Q" connoisseur, but I can sure eat some chocolate cake!)

Since my visit to Killen's, I have recommended it to many other people.

Maybe the first step you need to take in sharing your faith is to go to your favorite restaurant and enjoy your favorite meal. Think about all the reasons you love the place and the food. Notice how it affects you emotionally. Then ask Jesus to help you, through the Holy Spirit, experience a five-star life in Him so that you can easily, and more joyfully, begin recommending Him to others!

Chapter Work:
Five Stars

1. When was the last time you recommended a book, movie, restaurant, or contractor to someone else? On a scale of one to five, with five being the best, how would you rate whatever you recommended? How many stars does something, or someone, have to receive from you before you recommend it/them?

2. As you consider the life of Jesus, how many stars would you give His life? How many stars would you give your life? If your star-rating is low for either, spend time in prayer asking our Father to show you what keeps you from a higher rating. Be careful that you have not drifted, been lulled, into accepting a life less than what our Father has for you (John 10:10)!

3. How confident are you that in the gospel you genuinely have something of value, something helpful, to offer someone else? To the degree that you are not confident, will you ask our Father to fill in what you need so that your confidence will be complete?

4. Write a list of ten names of friends, family members, or co-workers that you know reasonably well. Without judgment, based on what you know of them, how would you rate their lives? What are the issues you encounter in the lives of other people? How challenging is it for you to see that all people are dealing with being separated from God and *need* to hear the gospel?

2 Story Power

FRANK WAS A junior in high school, well liked by his classmates. One day after school, he was at a good friend's house when the doorbell rang. This was one of those friends you have no problem answering the door for when their doorbell rings. So, Frank answered.

Two strangers were standing there. They greeted Frank and explained that they were out in the neighborhood sharing the love of Jesus Christ.

What the two visitors didn't know, and what Frank couldn't have fully realized, was how the Lord had been working to prepare the seventeen-year-old for this doorbell moment. Heading into that afternoon, all Frank knew was that he was going to hang out at his friend's house like he'd done many times before. Then the bell rang, right when Frank's friend was in the back of the house so that Frank would be the one to open the door.

While Frank can't remember the specifics of the visitors' words, thirty-two years later he does remember, "Something about what they were saying connected with something in me that was waking up."

And that day, there on the doorstep of his friend's house, Frank gave his life to Jesus and was saved.

Two people who loved the Lord spent an afternoon going door-to-door to share Jesus, not having any idea to whom the Lord would lead them. They could have been doing a thousand other things, but they chose to spread the news of Jesus.

This is God our Father working to reach people He loves through people He loves.

Frank has a very cool story of how he came to know Jesus! Hearing married couples tell how their paths crossed, how they fell in love, how they knew "This is the one I'm going to marry" is joyful.

I read one the other day about a fourteen-year-old guy who met a girl his age and knew he wanted to marry her. When he was sixteen, he asked the young lady's dad for permission to date her. Just after they turned eighteen, they married. They have been married more than fifty years!

Stories of how people surrender to Jesus can be just as memorable. What's your story of coming to know Jesus? What was happening in your life? How did God reach you?

I've never heard a boring conversion story. I've heard people tell what they thought was a boring story until I started asking questions—and then they came alive. There are no ho-hum conversion stories. However you were saved, it is a tale of love, sacrifice, pursuit, surrender, change, struggle, and LIFE. What's boring about that?

In fact, the easiest, most effective tool you have in sharing the gospel is your story. What's more personal to you than how our Father wooed and won you to Himself? You know more about your story than anyone else, which means you can freely, confidently share it without fear that you're going to be proven wrong. No one is going to overturn what you say. You are the authority, the expert, on your experience!

The apostle Peter counseled his disciples to be ready with their stories. He wrote 1 Peter to a group of persecuted Christians who had been scattered throughout Asia Minor (modern-day Turkey). These men and women were suffering greatly solely because they believed in Jesus. Peter reminded them:

> Even if you should suffer for the sake of righteousness, you are blessed. And do not fear their intimidation, and do not be troubled, but sanctify Christ as Lord in your hearts, always being ready to make a defense to everyone who asks you to give an account for the hope that is in you, yet with gentleness and reverence. (3:14–15)

The phrase "make a defense" means being able to explain to others how they could be hope-filled while enduring these trials. Peter wanted his brothers and sisters in the faith to be ready to share, through their individual stories, how and why Jesus was the source of their hope.

Because of Jesus, these Christians had hope. Because of this hope, they were genuinely optimistic about their lives despite significant persecution.

Our Christ-given stories of hope despite physical circumstances are equally powerful in our day and age. No one is immune to the struggles of life. For someone to truly live the hope of Jesus is to declare the love and faithfulness of our Father in the midst of a broken world. How does anybody do that? A life like that has a story to tell!

Are you ready to share your story about Jesus? Are you able to comfortably tell anyone who asks about the difference Jesus has made, and is making, in your life?

At some point you encountered *Christ*. Not an idea. Not a philosophy. Not a concept. You encountered *Jesus Christ* through the Holy Spirit.

You said yes.

You were brought from death to life.

You were moved from despair to hope.

That means you have a great story to tell!

WHAT HAPPENED?!

Kenny was raised in a denomination that doesn't emphasize the work of the Holy Spirit. Still, he loves Jesus and has walked in faith for more than forty years.

In 2015, he and I were on a group mission trip to Cuba. He had just finished sharing the gospel with a family in their home when a woman came up to him needing prayer. Through a translator, she informed Kenny of some pain she was having in her shoulder. As Kenny prayed, the woman grabbed his hand and placed it on the spot of her pain. When his hand touched her shoulder, Kenny felt something move through him and into her. He describes it this way: "A VERY strong, clear current of what I can only describe as electricity began to flow from my *arms* and *hands*! It was truly emotional and comforting to both of us."

By the time Kenny was done praying, the woman was overcome with joy. Her pain was gone! God our Father had just used Kenny as His instrument to supernaturally heal this woman.

Kenny's internal the-Holy-Spirit-does-not-do-this-today circuits were smoking! He came back to the group ecstatic and bewildered at what had just happened.

For the sake of training, let's slow down his experience.

A woman was experiencing physical pain, meaning the nerves in her body were having a negative reaction. She directed Kenny's hand to the place where she was hurting. The Holy Spirit moved through Kenny's arm and hand into the woman's shoulder, calming her nerves and restoring her health. The Holy Spirit changed a physical condition.

Can you envision the Holy Spirit moving in that way, from one person to another? Can you envision the relief on the woman's face as her shoulder pain subsided? Can you envision the joy of the Holy Spirit as He worked through Kenny to reach this dear woman whom the Father loves? That is awesome!

Now, let's take the same "slow-down approach" to your salvation story.

Before you gave your life to Jesus, you were separated from God and marked as His enemy. You lived your life the way you wanted, with no regard for God's plans and desires for you. Your spirit was diseased with sin. Think about a picture of a healthy lung versus a picture of a chain smoker's lung, but instead of a smoker's lung, you had a sinner's spirit. Had you died in that condition, you would have been condemned to eternal torment, apart from your Creator.

At some point, though, you heard about Jesus. Someone shared the gospel with you. Their words passed from their mouth into your ears. Those words traveled the length of your ear canal—from outer to inner ear (the cochlea). The cochlea has thousands of tiny hairs that translate auditory vibrations into electrical signals. These signals are then transferred by the auditory nerve to the brain. (I want to believe that when the hairs of my cochlea transmitted the gospel, they started partying!) As soon as the gospel hit your brain, you began to process the information. You were given a choice to receive Jesus or reject Him. At that fork in the road on the path of your life, you . . . said . . . YES! In the moment you said yes, many things happened:

- *God our Father wiped away every one of your sins.* His record of your life was instantly changed. He had a ledger with your name on it that was continually filling up with your sins against Him, for which He was going to hold you accountable. When you said yes, that ledger was erased and replaced with the life of Jesus.[1]
- *The Holy Spirit moved in.* Jesus said in John 3:5 that we must be born by the Spirit. When you said yes, the Holy Spirit took up residence inside of you. Slow it

---
[1] 1 John 4:10.

down. Watch Him move, crossing the barrier of who you are to dwell within you.

- *Your spirit was healed, made alive.* When the Holy Spirit moved in, He removed your diseased spirit and you were born again spiritually.[2] Again, you have to slow it down to appreciate the miracle. Your diseased spirit was made new again. Can you see the change in you?
- *You were adopted into the family of God.* Until that point, you were not a child of God. In the moment you said yes, you were brought into our Father's family. Can you see your adoption taking place? You say yes. The Holy Spirit comes in. He makes you alive, and instantly you are welcomed inside your heavenly Father's family, no longer a stranger, an enemy, or an outsider.[3]
- *You were rescued.* Paul explained in Colossians 1:13–14 that until God "transferred us to the kingdom of His beloved Son, in whom we have redemption, the forgiveness of sins," we were living in temporal darkness with a one-way ticket to eternal darkness. But then you and I were rescued. Can you see that in the moment you said yes, you accepted the outstretched hand of Jesus, your Rescuer? The use of *rescue* isn't a literary device to help us understand some other reality that occurred. No. You were literally rescued by Jesus in that moment!

---

[2] John 3:3; Romans 8:10.
[3] John 1:12–13; Galatians 4:4–7.

Every one of these events is an absolute miracle. Every one of them was supernatural. And, if you have given your life to Jesus, every one of them has happened to you!

You have a story to tell. Slow down your story.

- How did you hear about Jesus?
- Why did you say yes?
- Where were you?
- How did you get there?
- What happened inside you as you heard?
- Was that the first time you'd heard the gospel or had you heard some or all of it before?
- If it wasn't your first hearing, why do you think you said yes this time?

If you've given your life to Jesus, there's incredible poetry in your story. There is spiritual rhythm in all that our Father was doing to pursue you, reach you, invite you, woo you, and win you.

Every conversion story is a miracle.

You have a miracle story to tell.

STORY POWER

Few biblical accounts demonstrate story power like John 9.

Jesus and His disciples are in Jerusalem when they "happen upon" a man blind from birth. The disciples rationalize that this man's blindness must be the consequence of his or his parents' sin. Of course, the disciples are wrong again. Jesus corrects them, "It was neither that this man sinned, nor his parents; but it was so that the works of God might be displayed in him" (verse 3). Then Jesus applied clay (from His spittle mixed with dirt) to the man's eyes and sent him to wash in the pool of Siloam. The man came back seeing!

Let's slow this down to capture more of the miracle. When the man was washing the clay off in the pool, the Holy Spirit moved to heal whichever part of his eye had caused his blindness. Given Jesus' explanation to His disciples, this man probably had a birth defect in which his optic nerve did not form correctly, derailing the transfer of data from the eyes to the brain. When the Holy Spirit healed him, the Spirit touched the blind man's optic nerve.

For the first time in his life, light entered the man's eyes and connected to his brain. He could see!

He had a story to tell!

The people in his community knew who he was—he was the blind beggar guy. But now the blind guy could see! They were astonished.

"How then were your eyes opened?" they asked (verse 10).

He replied, "The man who is called Jesus made clay, and anointed my eyes, and said to me, 'Go to Siloam and wash'; so I went away and washed, and I received sight" (verse 11).

The miracle caught the attention of the Pharisees, the religious leaders of the day. They investigated the miraculous claim, confused as to how this man was healed and angry that he was healed on the Sabbath. (Jews observed the Sabbath on Saturday, a day of complete rest in which even healings were not allowed.) The Pharisees interviewed the formerly blind man twice. All the guy did was continue to tell his story.

During their second interrogation, the Pharisees demanded that the man acknowledge Jesus as a sinner for violating their Sabbath law. Now, remember, the Pharisees were far more learned in religion than this "simpleton." They had drawn him into a theological confrontation for which he was woefully ill-equipped and severely outmanned. Did he panic? Did he run away? Did he tremble? No. No. And no. He just stuck to his story: "Whether He is a sinner, I do not know; one thing I do know, that though I was blind, now I see" (verse 25).

The Pharisees were furious. They were also stumped. Like Superman's X-ray vision or Wonder Woman's lasso of truth, story power is a superpower. The man unloaded story power, and these "wise" and "venerable" religious leaders were left confounded.

"He shared his personal testimony. Simple. Straightforward. Bold," remarks Pastor Charles Stanley. "How often do we simply tell that we were once blind to the truth of Christ and now we see? That's really what people want to know. They aren't asking deep theological questions. They just want to know what happened in our lives that makes us different."[4]

When you are confident about your story, you can stand in front of anyone. You don't have to worry about being theologically outmatched; it won't matter if there are twenty of them and one of you. You won't ever be without an answer.

Just tell your story.

Resist the lies that you have nothing to share, or you don't know what you're talking about, or you're going to look foolish.

---

[4] Charles F. Stanley, *The Glorious Journey* (Nashville, TN: Thomas Nelson, 1996), Logos Bible e-book edition.

You have your story. Story power enabled an uneducated man to stare down the elite of his day. It will also enable you to GO and succeed no matter who you meet.

EFFECTIVE STORYTELLING

Neuroscientists continue to discover the effect that storytelling has on our brains. Paul J. Zak is the founding director of the Center for Neuroeconomics Studies and a professor of economics, psychology, and management at Claremont Graduate University. In an article he published in the *Harvard Business Review*, he wrote about his laboratory's attempts to "hack" the body's oxytocin system to see if people could be more motivated to cooperate with others. (Oxytocin is a neurochemical that signals that someone is "safe," and therefore we can move closer to them.)

Zak explained their experiment:

> To do this, we tested if narratives shot on video, rather than face-to-face interactions, would cause the brain to make oxytocin. By taking blood draws before and after the narrative, we found that character-driven stories do consistently cause oxytocin synthesis. Further, the amount of oxytocin released by the brain predicted how much people were willing to help others; for example, donating money to a charity associated with the narrative.[5]

---

[5] Paul J. Zak, "Why Your Brain Loves Good Storytelling," *Harvard Business Review*, October 28, 2014, https://hbr.org/2014/10/why-your-brain-loves-good-storytelling/.

Simply put, effective storytelling changes our brain chemistry, leading us to engage with both the story and the teller. Every time I read the man-born-blind story in the Gospel of John, I find myself cheering for him and against the Pharisees. When he stumps them, I find myself thinking, *Take that, you bunch of religious elites!*

So, what does it take to tell an effective story? Certainly, not all stories are the same. How many have you heard that start great but go so long that your mind drifts? When we tell our stories, we want to tell them well.

There are three elements to the former blind man's story—the past, the result, and the cause.

- **The Past:** *I once was blind.*
- **The Result:** *Now I see.*
- **The Cause:** *Jesus did it.*

First, talk about your past. What are the issues and sins you've battled? You certainly don't have to share every detail, or very many details, but give a clear picture of who you were. Just don't dwell there. You want to spend the bulk of your story on the cause and result. I regularly tell people, "Before Jesus, I was heavily into sex, drugs, and rock 'n' roll." I usually don't have to offer more details. But when it is helpful—such as when I'm talking to someone who has been deeply involved in a similar lifestyle—I do.

Then talk about Jesus. Share how you gave your life to Him. Remember, you are sharing with someone who has never had this experience. I didn't grow up in church, and so I had very little understanding of Jesus. I would've been clueless had someone not explained to me His story and how salvation works.

Lastly, tell your listener about your transformation. What ongoing changes have you experienced in your life because of Jesus? What impact did giving your life to Him have on the issues you were battling? Give a clear description of your before and after. One helpful exercise to guide your perspective is to consider who you would have become had Jesus not entered your life.

You don't have to use the elements in the same order. You can easily say: *Jesus changed my life* [Cause]. *I can see now* [Result]. *I used to be blind* [Past]. Or . . . *I can see now* [Result]. *Jesus* [Cause] *healed my blindness* [Past]. As long as you have the three aspects in your story, you are set up for effective telling.

We need to consider two other aspects of effective storytelling: *clarity* and *time*. I regularly come across people with dynamic stories, but when they tell theirs, the story line is all over the place, making it difficult to follow. Other tellers I meet haven't thought through how to share what God has done. In all my years of public speaking, I have learned that knowing something in our heads doesn't necessarily mean we can get it out of our mouths. So once you've finished reading this chapter, I want you to take time to think through your story. Write it down. When I work with preachers, I ask them to manuscript their sermons. They don't like it! But manuscripting forces you to work through exactly what you want to say. Besides, if you can't tell your story clearly, how can you expect anyone to understand it or to keep listening?

Time-wise, I remember watching the first *Lord of the Rings* movie, *The Fellowship of the Ring*, and wondering if it was ever going to end. It was a great story that I thought (and hoped) was going to wrap up five times before it concluded at the 3:48 mark (that's three *hours*, forty-eight *minutes*)!

How do you feel when the one telling a story—any story—goes on too long? How about when a pastor preaches too long? No matter how great your content is, going too long can kill your effectiveness.

Conversely, if you stop short and people want more, they will let you know! Too short is always better than too long. You need to be able to tell your story in any amount of time, whether that is forty-five seconds or thirty minutes.

Philippians 3:4–11 is one of several places[6] in the Bible where the apostle Paul tells his story. As you read through these verses, note how he communicates the past, the cause, and the result—and does so with clarity and conciseness.

> If someone else thinks they have reasons to put confidence in the flesh, I have more: circumcised on the eighth day, of the people of Israel, of the tribe of Benjamin, a Hebrew of Hebrews; in regard to the law, a Pharisee; as for zeal, persecuting the church; as for righteousness based on the law, faultless.
>
> But whatever were gains to me I now consider loss for the sake of Christ. What is more, I consider everything a loss because of the surpassing worth of knowing Christ Jesus my Lord, for whose sake I have lost all things. I consider them

---

[6] See also Acts 22:1–21, where Paul tells his story to a crowd of hostile Jews; Acts 26:1–32, where Paul shares his story with King Agrippa; and Galatians 1:11—2:21, where Paul recounts his story to the Galatians in defense of his ministry.

garbage, that I may gain Christ and be found in him, not having a righteousness of my own that comes from the law, but that which is through faith in Christ—the righteousness that comes from God on the basis of faith. I want to know Christ—yes, to know the power of his resurrection and participation in his sufferings, becoming like him in his death, and so, somehow, attaining to the resurrection from the dead. (NIV)

That is story power on display. Short, evocative, clear . . . and written down.

WHAT ABOUT THE JENNYS?

I was a student pastor at a church in Pearland, Texas, from 2001 to 2005. In that first year, I met Jenny, who was in the ninth grade and who already possessed a strong love for the Lord. She became a main leader in our ministry. Later, she went on to get her doctorate in physical therapy.

Unlike many of her peers, Jenny never wavered in her faith as she got older. She never rebelled. Now in her thirties, Jenny recalls giving her life to Jesus as Savior at age five and then truly identifying Jesus as Lord when she was eleven or twelve years old. So she doesn't have a dramatic sex-drugs-rock-and-roll/I-was-blind-and-now-I-see account. How does she tell her story?

> I remember being at a camp in high school when I saw one of our youth group members who was known to be into drugs, and my heart was filled with judgment. The Lord impressed upon me that while I hadn't taken part in those same external

sins, my heart struggled with many deep-rooted sins that were in need of just as much of His grace, healing, and forgiveness. God reminded me that "man looks at the outward appearance but the Lord looks at the heart" [1 Samuel 16:7].

God began to show me that while I may not have sinned outwardly like this student had, I do have a heart that rebels against Him. I struggle with perfectionism and pride that has no room for grace. Just because someone cannot see it outwardly doesn't mean I'm not guilty of it inwardly. I have plenty of internal struggles that He sees and knows—but He is so good and does not abandon me. Instead, He patiently heals and transforms my brokenness as I surrender it to Him.

Over the years, through joys and grief, hardship and doubt, the characteristic of God that most woos my heart is His beautiful grace—for each moment, in all circumstances. It's the grace that is offered to ALL mankind in our brokenness, no matter the perceived magnitude of sin.

Do you see the power of storytelling? Whether you are a John 9 man-born-blind or a Jenny, God our Father pursued you and invited you into a healing, loving, never-ending relationship with Him. Whatever circumstances led to your conversion, they are miraculous. The slow-motion replay of your salvation, your rescue, is miraculous.

You have story power!

Take time to clarify it first.

Practice it with friends.

Then go and share what Jesus has done.

Chapter Work:
Story Power

1. Do you believe you are a walking miracle? How well do you know your story of coming to faith in Jesus? If you have never written your story, take some time and do so now. You will be amazed at how writing your story will help inspire you to share your story with others.

2. Reflect on the miracle of what happened to you when you were saved. Reflect on the significance of your baptism. These are significant events in your new life that demonstrate our Father's love, work, and faithfulness.

3. Are you a Jenny or a man born blind? If you are a Jenny and struggle to tell your story, ask the Holy Spirit to show you how His power has been actively at work in you. While your story may not include an "I once was blind and now I see" experience, your transformation is just as miraculous and you have a powerful story to flex!

3 A Clear and Present Benefit

I WROTE THIS SPECIFIC chapter in March of 2020, just as governments around the world were announcing lockdowns due to the coronavirus outbreak. At the same time that the state and federal governments were issuing restrictions and business closings here in America, I saw followers of Jesus posting verses on social media that offered specific benefits of being in relationship with the Lord in times of uncertainty. Countering the anxiety, people posted Philippians 4:6–7. Countering fear, people posted 2 Timothy 1:7. For those in need of peace, John 14:27. For those in need of hope, 1 Peter 1:13. The intent was clear: there is real impact, real benefit, to walking with the Lord.

Before God called me into vocational ministry, I worked for a staffing company. As a recruiter, my job was to find exceptional employees for exceptional employers. One factor potential employees always asked about was the benefits package. In addition to their hourly rate or salary, they wanted clarity on what else they would be receiving.

Companies have long known the need to offer competitive, often creative, benefits packages if they hope to recruit and retain motivated staff. Consider these examples from a 2019 *Business News Daily* article:

- The Institute for Integrative Nutrition offers free weekly yoga and massages.
- At Netflix headquarters, hours worked and vacation time are not tracked. All that matters is getting work done.
- Deloitte offers new moms and dads up to sixteen weeks of paid time off and will reimburse up to $25,000 of expenses for adoption or surrogacy.
- Patagonia encourages its staff to surf and provides on-site bikes, volleyball courts, and yoga.[1] (I wonder if Patagonia needs a staff chaplain?)

Everyone wants to know about benefits. Benefits like these are real pluses that people can see themselves using.

The same is true when people are hearing about Jesus. They want to know: What are the benefits? Why should I do this? What will I get out of this?

While these questions may at first seem uncomfortable or self-serving, they're critical to successfully reaching people who

---

[1] Katharine Paljug, "16 Cool Job Perks That Keep Employees Happy," updated June 18, 2020, https://www.businessnewsdaily.com/5134-cool-job-benefits.html/.

don't believe in Jesus. In fact, when you came to faith in Jesus, you did so because you discovered, or were shown, a real and true benefit to surrendering. And as your faith has grown, you've experienced more and more benefits in Him.

In the previous chapters, we've talked about your story and its power. But I don't want you to limit what you share with others to your conversion experience. As you walk with Jesus, He fills page after page of your life with incredible blessings. You'll have an ongoing story with Him, just as you do with other close relationships. So let's focus here on drawing out the specific benefits you enjoy *because* of Jesus. I want you to be able to easily share those benefits with anyone anywhere.

THE KINGDOM-BENEFITS PLAN

To be in relationship with the Father, Son, and Holy Spirit is to experience a new way of life that comes with a tremendous benefits plan. Ancient Israel's King David, who penned so many biblical psalms, meditated frequently on the Lord's benefits and the impact of God's presence in his life. In Psalm 103:1-5, David wrote:

> Bless the LORD, O my soul,
> And all that is within me, bless His holy name.
> Bless the LORD, O my soul,
> *And forget none of His benefits*;
> Who pardons all your iniquities,
> Who heals all your diseases;
> Who redeems your life from the pit,

> Who crowns you with lovingkindness and compassion;
> Who satisfies your years with good things,
> So that your youth is renewed like the eagle.

David was essentially blessing the Lord because of the benefits package he enjoyed by being in relationship with Him. Then the poet-king highlighted the benefits, which included forgiveness, healing, redemption, love, compassion, and satisfaction. This is certainly not a complete list of the advantages David experienced, but it is an extraordinary list. He finished his "inventory" by giving a clear, evocative, exciting picture that anyone can experience in relationship with the Lord: having "your youth . . . renewed." Who doesn't want that?

Notice how David itemized real, practical benefits of a relationship with God. These weren't irrelevant things in David's life. He was articulating features of the relationship that had been vitally important to him.

David wasn't the only one who spoke of benefits. Consider some of the many benefits that Jesus mentioned to His audiences. The kingdom of heaven offers

- worry-free living as God the Father takes responsibility for daily provision (Matthew 6:25–33).
- eternal life (7:13–14).
- an indestructible life that can endure any storm (7:24–27).
- forgiveness of sins (9:1–8).
- the experience of divine love (John 3:16).

Jesus offers

- family (Mark 10:28–31).
- treasure in heaven (Luke 18:18–27).
- the benefit of being born again (John 3:4–21).
- life today (5:39–40; 10:10).

Again, these are not exhaustive lists. I simply wanted you to see that in His evangelism and teaching, Jesus regularly spoke of relevant, legitimate benefits. He never said, "Follow Me just because."

When John sat down to write his Gospel, it's apparent that he reflected on what was meaningful to him in his relationship with Christ. The apostle desired to clearly articulate those benefits so that people would believe in Jesus and have the opportunity to experience the same advantages. John summarized the point of his Gospel in 20:30–31: "Many other signs Jesus also performed in the presence of the disciples, which are not written in this book; but these have been written so that you may believe that Jesus is the Christ, the Son of God; and that believing *you may have life* in His name."

To accomplish this purpose, John structured his Gospel around seven "I AM" statements of Jesus. Seven times the Son of God definitively declared that He can provide very specific benefits to those who would follow Him:

- *I am the bread of life.* The souls of believers are nourished. We no longer have to feed on the emptiness of the world (6:35).

- *I am the Light of the world.* Followers of Christ can see with divine wisdom. They are freed from only seeing the gray and the haze (8:12).
- *I am the door of the sheep.* We access the Lord's pasture and are released from the burden of seeking pasture in the world (10:7, 9).
- *I am the good shepherd.* As Jesus' sheep, we receive divine guidance and direction, which relieves us of having to figure out life on our own (10:11, 14).
- *I am the resurrection and the life.* Our lives are secure for eternity, freed from fear and uncertainty about what happens to us when we die (11:25).
- *I am the way, and the truth, and the life.* In Him we have an undefeatable example, absolute reliability, and an abundance that cannot be found anywhere else (14:6).
- *I am the true vine.* Jesus' disciples experience an unending supply of all that we need for life. We do not have to generate our own supply (15:1, 5).

John's goal in capturing these "I AM" statements was to reveal different benefits to life in Jesus. You cannot share Jesus without sharing His benefits.

BECAUSE OF JESUS

At a men's retreat, I asked everyone who was in sales to raise their hands. There were a half dozen of these professionals in the room.

I asked each salesman to tell us the name of his company, the industry his employer was in, and the competitive advantage his company offered. Playing the role of the customer, I wanted to know what benefit I would receive if I used his company's product or service.

One man said, "Efficiency. We can get product to you more efficiently than our competitors, which allows you to get to market faster."

Another remarked, "Our company outdoes our competitors by providing far better customer service. Our industry thrives on plants operating at full capacity. Plants have issues. The company with the best customer service wins. We win."

Each sales guy quickly, clearly, and confidently named the distinct benefits of their company.

We humans like benefits. We like to know, "What's in it for me?" We want to do business with companies that can give us a personal advantage. As a Christian, you experience powerful, practical benefits in your life *because* of Jesus. What are they?

If you say one of those benefits is "eternal life," then I want to hear how that improves your life today. Maybe your enduring future with God is something you think about regularly; the assurance of your place in heaven gives you daily peace. If that's true in your everyday experience, then that's powerful. But if you suggest "eternal life" as a benefit and it doesn't affect your daily experience, then I want to hear about benefits that *do* impact you.

For example, I know a guy named Greg who used to be crushed by anxiety. After coming to faith in Jesus, he learned how to take specific issues like this to his Father in heaven. Greg's anxiety completely disappeared. He became a man at peace. He recently sent me this text:

"Wanted to get some good coffee and went to my usual spot. [The barista] started telling me about his anxiety so I asked how he deals w it. Then got to tell him how Jesus radically changed the way I face anxiety . . . and away we go!"[2]

Do you see my point? Dealing with anxiety is a clear, present benefit that Greg enjoys because of Jesus. This is something he can easily, confidently, share with others. And because it's so practical, Greg has plenty of instances to recount that demonstrate how his Jesus-centered approach to anxiety works.

Three of the primary benefits I enjoy because of Jesus are *direction*, *wisdom*, and *power from above*. Thanks to Him, I'm able to learn and follow the will of God. I don't have to worry whether I'm in the right place. I have deep joy in knowing that I'm following the One who is undefeatable.

I love Psalm 16:7–11, specifically verse 11, where David wrote, "You will make known to me the path of life; in Your presence is fullness of joy; in Your right hand there are pleasures forever." Then, in Psalm 25:10, David said: "All the paths of the Lord are lovingkindness and truth to those who keep His covenant and His testimonies." Many other passages of Scripture, as well as the lives of biblical men and women, testify to the benefit of following God's direction. Pastor A. W. Tozer wrote, "God is directing His people in the way He wants them to go. Often it is not the way we want to go, but as we yield ourselves to God, He opens doors and leads us forward."[3] Tozer understood the

---

[2] Personal correspondence with author via text, September 16, 2020.
[3] A. W. Tozer, *A Cloud by Day, a Fire by Night: Finding and Following God's Will for You* (Bloomington, MN, Bethany House, 2019), 14.

importance of following God's direction. It's a powerful benefit of knowing God.

In addition to the Lord's leadership, I enjoy His wisdom. God gives me insight into how life and relationships work. My wife and I recently had an issue with one of our children. We weren't sure what to do. We prayed and waited for the Holy Spirit to speak into the situation. And He did. We are keenly aware that we're unable to parent our kids apart from the indwelling wisdom of the Holy Spirit. And, because we access His wisdom, we get the benefit of knowing that we are parenting according to the Lord! I have no idea where other parents get their confidence.

Jesus promised, "I will ask the Father, and He will give you another Helper, that He may be with you forever; that is the Spirit of truth, whom the world cannot receive, because it does not see Him or know Him, but you know Him because He abides with you and will be in you."[4] The Holy Spirit is my Helper. What is He helping me to do? To know and understand how to live faithfully with my Father. Parenting is included in that! Additionally, I'm convinced that God my Father wants me to be a far better father to my children than I ever could be on my own. So I'm actively walking in the unsurpassed benefit of the Holy Spirit.

I was with a friend who was struggling to develop a parenting strategy for his son, who has ADHD (attention deficit hyperactivity disorder). I suggested he and his wife pray and ask the Holy Spirit to give them a way forward. I also shared with him what

---

[4] John 14:16–17.

parenting in the benefit of the Spirit looks like for me and my wife. Story with a specific benefit!

Power from above is a third benefit that I enjoy each day. I constantly battle varying forms of negativity. Receiving a phone call from a big-name businessperson can make me feel arrogant. The very next phone call, informing me about an unexpected financial hit, can depress me if I'm not sure how we will pay that bill. Then I eat lunch and I'm tempted with gluttony. I read the news and I battle feelings of anger. I watch television and am tempted to lust. And on and on . . .

All of these attacks have power. Yet I'm super grateful that in Christ I have surpassing power! I regularly exercise the power of Christ in me against sin, the world, and Satan. These enemies actively work to destroy my faith. Here are power verses that strengthen me from 1 Corinthians 2:

> I was with you in weakness and in fear and in much trembling, and my message and my preaching were not in persuasive words of wisdom, but in demonstration of the Spirit and of power, so that your faith would not rest on the wisdom of men, but on the power of God. (verses 3–5)

I'm continually learning how to rest my faith in the power of God! Thanks to what I've learned so far, I've already experienced so much breakthrough and daily victory that it keeps me coming back for more.

Direction, wisdom, and power from above are part of my kingdom-benefit plan that I love to tell others about. What are yours? Sit with the Lord and ask Him to show you. Write down what you get most out of walking with Jesus. Rehearse those benefits. Talk about them with your spouse, your good friend, your small group or Bible study group.

You aren't walking with Jesus for nothing. More than likely, the benefits you enjoy the most track with the deepest pain and struggle you've experienced. Don't discount or minimize the great and wonderful works our Father has done and is doing in you. David proclaimed, "Many, O Lord my God, are the wonders which You have done, and Your thoughts toward us; there is none to compare with You. If I would declare and speak of them, they would be too numerous to count."[5]

ANCHORS AWEIGH

The USS *Gerald R. Ford* is the largest aircraft carrier in the world. Commissioned in 2017, the ship is 1,092 feet long with a 256-foot-wide flight deck that can hold 75 aircraft. With 100,000 long tons of full load displacement and the ability to transport approximately 4,550 soldiers at a time,[6] this carrier is an incredible specimen that will serve the United States Navy for decades to come.

You can imagine a ship that size would need an enormous anchor to secure its position in every type of water.

The anchor weighs 30,000 pounds.

The anchor chain is 1,440 feet long.

---

[5] Psalm 40:5.
[6] "Ready for the 21st Century," *All Hands*, accessed January 10, 2021, https://allhands.navy.mil/Features/Ford/.

Each link weighs 136 pounds.[7]

The anchor and chain are so enormous that once deployed, the *Gerald R. Ford* is not going anywhere! Whether it's the wind topside or the undercurrent below, nothing is going to budge the *Ford* when her anchor is sunk.

You also face powerful forces in life, both external and internal, that are trying to dislodge you from your faith. Kingdom benefits are robust and rich. Scripture can be a 30,000-pound anchor that secures your life to God's blessings and becomes a part of your storytelling.

In the previous section, I connected my benefits to Scripture. My benefits are not just things I get to enjoy because I have some special sort of relationship with God; the Bible directly attests to them. They are my anchor. I can confidently share them because they are definitively stated in God's Word, which means they are absolutely reliable in real life. My life testifies to the truth and trustworthiness of the Bible.

Remember my friend Kenny-the-healer from the previous chapter? One of the great benefits he receives because of Jesus is the gift of contentment. He LOVES to talk about how Jesus teaches him to be content. His anchor verse is Philippians 4:12: "I know how to get along with humble means, and I also know how to live in prosperity; in any and every circumstance I have learned the secret of being filled and going hungry, both of having abundance and suffering need." His contentment is connected to God's Word.

---

[7] Kyle Mizokami, "You Don't Want to Get in the Way of a 100,000-Ton Aircraft Carrier's Anchor," *Popular Mechanics*, October 19, 2017, https://www.popularmechanics.com/military/navy-ships/a28701/uss-ford-anchor-test-video/.

One of the cool things about Kenny's anchor verse is that he is not a natural at memorizing Scripture. But you know what it's like when God connects His Word to your life? That is what the Lord did for Kenny with Philippians 4, and it's what He will do for you (if He hasn't already). Anchor verses are not the ones people struggle to remember; they're the ones we enjoy sharing!

Take time to sit quietly with the Lord. Identify three benefits. Don't overdo it and come up with ten. Start with three. Or, if three is too many, focus on one. Consider how faithful our Father is to you in that one area of your life. Be reminded of how constantly He provides. Next, connect each benefit to a passage of Scripture.[8] Ask the Holy Spirit to bring you to a place where you feel great about the benefits you have. Then pray that He will give you opportunities, and the courage, to share naturally with others.

---

[8] If this task sounds daunting, there are a number of Bible-search tools online that will help you connect your benefits with an anchor verse. BibleGateway.com and BlueLetterBible.org are good places to start.

Chapter Work:
A Clear and Present Benefit

List the three notable benefits you experience in your relationship with Jesus. Reflect on one story for each benefit. Write one Scripture passage that supports that benefit. For example, one of your benefits may be a victory in anxiety. You have regular stories of the Holy Spirit overcoming your anxious thoughts as you release specific triggers to our Father in Jesus' name. A meaningful scripture continues to be Philippians 4:6–7.

4 Attitude Check

BEN BUTLER RUNS an evangelistic ministry out of Harlingen, Texas, called Way of the Cross. In addition to the ministry's work on the US/Mexico border, Way of the Cross has extensive reach into the interior of Mexico and is the largest evangelistic ministry in Nicaragua. I've been on many crusade trips with Brother Ben all over Nicaragua. He is an awesome man who loves Jesus and loves seeing people be saved.

While on a Way of the Cross crusade, it's not unusual at any point to hear Brother Ben shout via megaphone, "Attitude check!" To which we all stop what we're doing and respond, "Praise the Lord!"

He replies, "How do you feel?" To which we laughingly respond, "Happy and blessed!"—and then we get back to hauling rice and beans, preaching, praying, or playing with kids.

I learned a long time ago from Ben that attitude in evangelism is far more important than technique. In evangelism, attitude is everything.

Many Christians are petrified of sharing Jesus with others. We don't want to be rejected. We're not sure what to say. We don't want to be labeled as a "Jesus freak." These fears paralyze us from actively reaching out to the lost with the eternal hope that is in Christ.

Consider these statistics from a 2019 study on evangelism from the Barna Group:

- Among Christian millennials, nearly half say it's wrong to evangelize.
- About four in ten practicing Christians say they have no non-Christian friends or family members.
- Fifty-six percent of believers report having two or fewer conversations about faith with a non-Christian during the past year.
- Perhaps most tellingly, the percentage who say "I would avoid discussions about my faith if my non-Christian friend would reject me" has risen from 33 to 44 percent in the past twenty-five years.
- Nine out of ten survey respondents agreed in 1993 that "every Christian has a responsibility to share their faith." Only two-thirds said the same in 2017.
- However willing they may be, a Christian's ability to witness for Christ may be impeded by the simple fact that they don't have meaningful connections with non-Christians or the conversational skills necessary to talk about issues of faith.[1]

---

[1] George Barna, *Reviving Evangelism: Current Realities That Demand a New Vision for Sharing Faith*, Barna.com (2019), PDF, https://shop.barna.com/products/reviving-evangelism?_ga=2.145078646.399236162.1605551856-500917807.1605551856/.

ATTITUDE CHECK

In other words, we need an attitude check.

So, how is your attitude toward GO-ing and sharing your faith in Jesus?

Sharing Jesus with others isn't a chore or an obligation—it's not like mowing the grass or doing dishes. So let me ask you, Why you are reading this book? It's commendable that you *are* reading this. According to the Barna Group, the majority of Christians never share their faith with others. So why are you pressing in? What's motivating you to take a step most Christians will never take?

A great deal of the work we are doing in *GO* has to do with a person's heart for reaching others. If you get your heart right, you'll be freed up to share Jesus in the rhythm of the Holy Spirit. If your heart is right, then you'll enjoy sharing Jesus and you'll look for opportunities to do so. So, let's start with a heart check. How is your attitude toward GO-ing?

Jesus taught that only one heart condition is right for His disciples: "If you love Me, you will keep My commandments."[2] He cares about our attitude in our "doing" for Him as much as, if not more than, He cares about what we actually do. Jesus doesn't want obligatory obedience. He wants obedience that flows naturally from a heart that loves Him. We learn to obey Jesus because we love Jesus.

So what is the right heart condition for making disciples? Love. By operating in love for those we are sharing with, our entire presence changes. Our tone changes. Our emotions change.

---

[2] John 14:15.

Look at the supremacy of love in the teaching of Paul in 1 Corinthians 13:

> If I speak with the tongues of men and of angels, but do not have love, I have become a noisy gong or a clanging cymbal. If I have the gift of prophecy, and know all mysteries and all knowledge; and if I have all faith, so as to remove mountains, but do not have love, I am nothing. And if I give all my possessions to feed the poor, and if I surrender my body to be burned, but do not have love, it profits me nothing. (verses 1–3)

That is an incredible list. How many of us would love to prophesy or move mountains? Certainly we could add "evangelize the nations" to the mix. Yet Paul says that if we do any or all of these things without love, our acts are rendered powerless.

Love makes the difference between a work of religion and a work in Jesus' name. So let's press into love and discover how it works as we GO.

SENT WITH LOVE

Something was gnawing at Nicodemus's soul. No matter how hard this Jewish religious leader tried, he couldn't shake the feeling that almost everything he believed and had worked for was being challenged. A new teacher had come out of Nazareth, of all places. (Everyone knew that nothing good came from there.)[3]

---
[3] John 1:46.

A new teacher with no formal training who wasn't part of the official temple leadership and who wasn't raised in the synagogue.[4] Nevertheless, His teaching had power. He was performing miracles and healing. Word on the street was that this man was even casting out demons!

Nicodemus was deeply conflicted.

One night, when Nicodemus couldn't stand the suspense any longer, he snuck away to find the one named Jesus. Nicodemus went by night because the group he belonged to, the Pharisees, strongly opposed Jesus. To be "caught" talking to this mysterious teacher privately would threaten a person's standing in the council. Still, Nicodemus had to have answers.

Jesus was happy to give him what he needed.

In their conversation, Jesus sought to convert Nicodemus from his current way of life. He began by telling the Pharisee that if he wanted to see the kingdom of God, he must be born again. Nicodemus struggled to understand what that meant, unaware that Jesus was talking about being spiritually born. In fact, Nicodemus was regularly tripped up by the spiritual elements of their conversation.[5]

At one point, Jesus explained God's motivation in sending Him to earth to preach the gospel. Why did God send Jesus as His first missionary? What was the Father's heart condition? His attitude? "For God so loved the world, that He gave His only begotten Son,

---

[4] Some Jewish writings from the early first centuries, and some verses from the Gospels, describe Jesus as a rabbi. In the first century, that term was used more informally than today. Many men at that time who taught or had followers were addressed as "Rabbi."
[5] John 3:1–21.

that whoever believes in Him shall not perish, but have eternal life,"[6] explained Jesus.

Love was the reason. When our Father considered each individual who would ever be created . . . when He envisioned you . . . He felt love. In love, our Father sent Jesus to evangelize the world, preaching the gospel in large groups, medium-sized groups, small groups, even one-on-one. The first missionary shared the life-changing, eternal, connecting, restoring news of the gospel. Because of love.

The apostle Paul understood the heart of God in making disciples, writing, "God demonstrates His own love toward us [you, me, and everyone else], in that while we were yet sinners, Christ died for us."[7] John offered this explanation: "By this the love of God was manifested in us, that God has sent His only begotten Son into the world so that we might live through Him. In this is love, not that we loved God, but that He loved us and sent His Son to be the propitiation [sufficient sacrifice] for our sins."[8]

The motive, the attitude, the heart condition of God our Father in evangelizing the world was love.

What do you love? I know people who love music. Music is just that thing that energizes them. Others love food. Some love sports. Or animals. Of course, those of us who are married love our spouses, and we parents love our kids. Think about what you love. How does that love *feel* to you?

---

[6] John 3:16.
[7] Romans 5:8.
[8] 1 John 4:9–10.

It is desire. You want to be doing those things you love. It is affection, joy, and electricity all wrapped into passion. There's no obligation, no burden. Rather, there is freedom. Love has a rhythm that feels natural. It compels you to dig deeper in order to understand more. You're content on the one hand, in that you're not looking for anything or anyone else to replace the object of your affection; on the other hand, you're not content because love induces you to want more and more of what you have. The one who loves sports isn't looking for some additional hobby; at the same time, their love for sports keeps them returning to sports every day. They want more and more.

This is what our Father feels—though purely, perfectly, and multiplied by infinity. As He thinks of you, He feels desire. He feels affection. He feels joy! He loves spending time with you!

Who doesn't love spending time with their children? Who doesn't look forward to seeing their kids? That is how your Father in heaven feels about you!

He loves you so much that He sent Jesus to reconnect you to Him. He loves you so much that He sent somebody to share Jesus with you. That person was a love messenger from our Father to you.

I shared my conversion story and the role Brett Russell played in my life in the introduction. Brett was the man God sent to me in 1996 because the Father in heaven loved me. Your evangelism story is your testimony of God our Father loving you and sending someone (or several someones) into your life. You being sent to GO and evangelize others will become part of *their* story of God our Father loving them.

Regardless of the technique or tool you use—whether you tell your story, apply Scripture, debate someone, share an EvangeCube or a gospel tract—your loving attitude can be the difference maker.

HOW DO I LOVE?

My son, Collin, asked me to help him understand our money supply in the US. He wanted to know the flow of money, from government printing to him getting it! *Ugh.* I tried to explain as best I could, but really, I stumbled around the topic a lot. When I finished, Collin responded, "That doesn't make any sense to me."

I had to laugh. My explanation didn't make any sense to me either!

I think I can do a better job of explaining how love works in making disciples. Admittedly, to truly love people we have never met sounds . . . odd. How can any of us be motivated by love to share Jesus with people we've never met? The answer is in the overflow of our Father's love for us.

Earlier in this chapter we looked at 1 John 4:9–10, where John described the love-motive of our Father in making disciples. The apostle continued teaching on this flow of love in verse 11: "Beloved, if God so loved us, we also ought to love one another." A few verses later, John wrote: "We have come to know and have believed the love which God has for us. God is love, and the one who abides in love abides in God, and God abides in him. . . . We love, because He first loved us" (verses 16, 19). Every bit of love we can have for others comes from the love we first received from our Father through the Son and the Holy Spirit.

There is a prerequisite, though. We can't love others until we first soak in God's love for us. We love because God first loved us.

The sequence works like this: First, God our Father draws you to Himself because He loves you. He sends someone to you who shares the gospel or their testimony. The Holy Spirit has already been working in you, awakening you to "heavenly things." As the Holy Spirit continues to move, you make the decision to receive that love and ask forgiveness for your sins so that you can then receive God's salvation.

Multiple things happen the moment you are saved:

- You are immediately forgiven of your sins, cleansed of your guilt, and filled with the righteousness of Jesus.
- You are born again, meaning that your spirit is now alive in Christ.
- You are filled with and sealed by the Holy Spirit, who mediates all the activity of Jesus and the Father in you.
- You are adopted into God our Father's family and instantly reconnected to your Creator.
- You receive a new name. Once you were an enemy; now you are a son or daughter.
- You are raised and seated with Christ "in the heavenly places, far above all rule and authority."[9]
- You are given citizenship in the kingdom of God.
- You are given a new destiny: the will of God for your life.

---

[9] Ephesians 1:20–21.

- You receive an eternal inheritance that can never be taken away from you.

All of this is yours because of love.

Second, as you experience your new, born-again life, you respond by loving your Father in heaven for opening your eyes to salvation and the wonder of life in Him. Your heart is ignited for Him, for Jesus, and for the Holy Spirit. God becomes your first love.

Third, you begin to love yourself for the first time. As you walk in the love of Jesus, you are changed. Paul wrote to the Christians in the city of Thessalonica, "We should always give thanks to God for you, brethren beloved by the Lord, because God has chosen you from the beginning for salvation through sanctification by the Spirit and faith in the truth."[10] "Sanctification" means transformation. To walk with Jesus is to be changed from whoever you were into who God created you to be in the likeness of Jesus.

In that divinely sanctifying work, you find yourself manifesting the fruit of the Spirit, which Paul listed in Galatians 5:22–23 as "love, joy, peace, patience, kindness, goodness, faithfulness, gentleness, self-control." As the Holy Spirit changes your character, you begin to feel better about yourself, to feel great about yourself, and, finally, to love yourself. You begin to feel great about being you!

Finally, in this love overflow, you can now GO, organically loving people you know and people you don't know. As you abide

---

[10] 2 Thessalonians 2:13.

in the all-consuming love of the Father, Son, and Holy Spirit, how you feel about other people will change. How you see other people will change.

A TRANSFORMATION STORY

God's transformation of the apostle Paul in Acts 9 is well known to many of us. On the way from Jerusalem to Damascus to persecute Christians, Paul (at the time known as Saul) was blinded by a vision of Jesus. Three days later, the scales that formed on Paul's eyes during his encounter fell off, and he began his new life in Christ, learning to see through the Spirit.

One of the effects of Paul's conversion was a change in the way he viewed people. Whereas before he saw with racist eyes—Jews were the chosen people of God; Gentiles were unworthy dogs—he began to proclaim, "From now on we recognize no one according to the flesh [outwardly]; even though we have known Christ according to the flesh, yet now we know Him in this way no longer."[11] Paul's eyes were changed so that he looked at people according to the Spirit, as one who walks in the love of our Father in heaven. His new sight compelled his evangelism: "Therefore, we are ambassadors for Christ, as though God were making an appeal through us; we beg you on behalf of Christ, be reconciled to God."[12]

Do you feel the urgency in Paul's language? His evangelism sprang from love—the urging of God the Father that people would repent and be reconciled through Paul's preaching.

---

[11] 2 Corinthians 5:16.
[12] 2 Corinthians 5:20.

Not only had Paul's view of Gentiles changed, but he saw Jews differently now as well.

> I am telling the truth in Christ, I am not lying, my conscience testifies with me in the Holy Spirit, that I have great sorrow and unceasing grief in my heart. For I could wish that I myself were accursed, separated from Christ for the sake of my brethren, my kinsmen according to the flesh, who are Israelites, to whom belongs the adoption as sons, and the glory and the covenants and the giving of the Law and the temple service and the promises.[13]

> Brethren, my heart's desire and my prayer to God for them is for their salvation.[14]

Before his conversion, Paul considered the Jews to be the chosen people of God, right in all they did. Then his heart and his sight were transformed so that he saw his brethren as lost, without the love of Jesus. His heart ached so strongly for them that if it would help their salvation for him to be "accursed," he would do it!

That is divinely powered love. You can feel Paul's yearning for those with whom he grew up. That is evangelism in the overflow. We can be motivated by love for people because we live in the continual outpouring of God's love for us.

That has been Kiwanya's experience. She was fourteen when she gave her life to Christ. Unfortunately, she drifted. By the time

---

[13] Romans 9:1–4.
[14] Romans 10:1.

she was thirty-two and came back to Jesus, she was a single mom. What she didn't know is that God was using her time in her "wilderness" to prepare her for a life in ministry.

As part of Kiwanya's restoration, the Lord began to change her heart and her eyes. He put a deep love in her for single women who were being released from prison. Before Kiwanya ever met any of the women she would come alongside, her heart burned with a love for them as they endured their challenging circumstances.

For more than twenty years, Kiwanya has been sharing the love of Jesus with women who leave prison. God's outpouring of love streams through her to them.

PURIFIED

John Maxwell, a top-selling Christian author known for his books on leadership and motivation, refers to our attitude as either "our best friend or our worst enemy."[15] We have seen that to be incredibly true when it comes to making disciples. If we have a bad attitude about sharing Jesus with others, we will never speak up. Our attitude is far more important in sharing Jesus for another reason. According to Maxwell, "People may *hear* your words, but they *feel* your attitude."[16]

Solomon understood God's desire for our attitude to be right when he wrote, "Every man's way is right in his own eyes, but the LORD weighs the hearts."[17] How do we get to a place where

---

[15] John C. Maxwell, *Motivated to Succeed: Inspirational Selections from John C. Maxwell* (Nashville, TN: Thomas Nelson, 2006), 11.
[16] John C. Maxwell, *Everyone Communicates, Few Connect: What the Most Effective People Do Differently* (Nashville, TN: Thomas Nelson, 2010), 65.
[17] Proverbs 21:2.

our attitude is purified so that we are going forth to reach others in love?

In the first place, don't wait. If you wait for your motive to be perfect, you'll never share Jesus with anyone. At one point while Paul was in prison, word came to him that some people were preaching Jesus for selfish gain. Paul responded, "What then? . . . Whether in pretense or in truth, Christ is proclaimed; and in this I rejoice."[18] God our Father can work salvation in others even if the one preaching is doing so selfishly! The urgency is to get the gospel out to the world.

As you are GO-ing, open your heart to the Lord and ask Him to purify your motive. Psalm 139:23–24 is an excellent passage for bringing your motives before the Lord: "Search me, O God, and know my heart; try me and know my anxious thoughts; and see if there be any hurtful way in me, and lead me in the everlasting way." The one who walks with the Lord humbly understands that he or she is continually in need of restoration and healing. We come to our Father with open hands, willing to have Him reveal our sinful motives.

When we are sensitive to the amount of forgiveness we need in our lives and how, in love, our Father readily forgives us through Jesus, then our hearts can be changed. The Holy Spirit works in us, as He did in Paul's transformation, to remake us into people of love.

So, do not wait for your motive to be 100 percent pure.

But do not hide your motive from the Lord.

---

[18] Philippians 1:18.

Watch your attitude toward those to whom our Father sends you. Do you feel love for the one who is different than you? Do you feel love for the one whose sin struggle is particularly repugnant to you? Do you feel love for the one you perceive would never want anything to do with Jesus?

Don't beat yourself up for your thoughts toward others; bring them before the Lord, repent of them, and ask Him to change you. Changing you into one who will love people is the work and desire of the Holy Spirit.

THE LESSON FROM EPHESUS

The church at Ephesus in Paul's time was a great church by many standards. The brothers and sisters there were fully engaged in fantastic ministry work. They stood strong against false teachers and false apostles. They persevered in the face of persecution. They had great outreach and benevolence programs, serving the Lord commendably.

But, they had one root flaw. The flaw was so severe, it threatened the life and effectiveness of the community. In fact, if the Christians at Ephesus did not correct this, Jesus threatened to come and "remove [their] lampstand out of its place."[19]

What was their flaw? Jesus said in Revelation 2:4, "I have this against you, that you have left your first love." While they had great ministry, they lost their love. They had fallen guilty to Paul's warning in 1 Corinthians 13:1: "If I speak with the tongues of men

---

[19] Revelation 2:5. The lampstand symbolized the presence and work of the Holy Spirit in the church. Jesus was threatening to remove the Holy Spirit from their fellowship.

and of angels, but do not have love, I have become a noisy gong or a clanging cymbal."

Being motivated by love is more important in sharing Jesus with others than any technique you can master. God our Father sent Jesus because of love. Jesus came to this earth because of love. God sends you out into the world with your story because of love. Let us open our hearts to the inner working of the Holy Spirit so that we can GO, like Jesus, because of love!

Chapter Work:
Attitude Check

1. Often we need significant work done in us concerning our attitude toward sharing our story with others. Write one word that summarizes your attitude toward GO-ing and sharing your faith in Jesus with others.

2. Our Father wants us to flex our stories from a heart of love just as He sent Jesus to us from His love. What difficulties do you have in being motivated by love?

3. In the divine sequence of love, we first receive love from the Father, Son, and Holy Spirit. Then, in response, we love them. Because in their love for us, they demonstrate our worth. And as they begin conforming us into the image of Jesus, we begin to love ourselves. In the overflow of the divine sequence, now we go and flex our stories in love. Reflect on the following:

    a. How regularly do you receive love from the Father, Son, and Holy Spirit? How do you encounter their love?

b. How do you regularly demonstrate your love for them?

c. How comfortable are you in loving yourself? Remember, Jesus' standard is not the way we merely feel okay about ourselves but that we love ourselves because of our Father's love in us.

Allow the Holy Spirit to bring healing or clarity to your heart as you consider what it means to flex your story in love.

4. Psalm 139:23–24 is an excellent passage to pray so that the Holy Spirit can continually heal you in your motives. Consider memorizing the passage. As you sit with our Father in those verses, note any additional words He wants to speak to you about the condition of your motives.

5 Don't Golf

I AM NOT A fan of golf. My dad loves the sport. At least, I think he loves it. He's been playing as long as I can remember.

When I was a kid, he would invite me to go with him and ride around in the cart. The cart was the only cool part. For four to five hours, my dad would huff and puff (and a whole bunch of other things!) at his results, and that left me wondering why he kept voluntarily doing this to himself week after week. Golf seemed ludicrous to me—why spend $70 or more for several hours of getting extremely mad at yourself?

No thank you.

Although most people golf with friends, golf is an individual sport: one person, by themselves, against the course. Players may have been coached in specific parts of their game, but when the first ball is teed up, everyone is on their own. One against all.

If you want to succeed in disciple-making and have a great time doing it, do not play golf! GO-ing is not a one-against-the-course effort. You don't receive instruction from a coach and then get sent onto the playing field to compete on your own. Jesus didn't do it that way, and He doesn't send us that way.

Part of the richness of Jesus' approach with His disciples is that He modeled what I call "Trinitarian GO-ing." In the first book of this series, *BE*, I walk through *Trinitarian intimacy*, the biblical teaching that when we give our lives to Jesus, we are brought into a healthy relationship with God the Father, God the Son, and God the Holy Spirit. While Scripture affirms that there is only one God in all of creation, Scripture also affirms that God exists in three persons who work in our lives in different ways.

In this chapter, we consider the impact of Trinitarian intimacy as we share the Good News with others.

A VERY BAD EXAMPLE

One account of sharing-Jesus-gone-wrong (found in Acts 19) is so terrible, it would go viral if it happened today.

The apostle Paul is spending two years in Ephesus during his third missionary journey. While he is there evangelizing, the Spirit of the Lord is winning souls and working incredible miracles, including delivering people from demonic possession. A man named Sceva, a Jewish chief priest, has seven sons who are Jewish exorcists. The sons of Sceva see Paul's great success and attempt to mimic his ministry. At one point, the biblical writer records them saying to a demon who had possessed someone, "I adjure you by Jesus whom Paul preaches" (verse 13). The evil spirit responds to the sons of Sceva, "I recognize Jesus, and I know about Paul, but who are you?" (verse 15).

What happens next is brutal. Scripture says the demon-possessed man beat up all seven sons, stripping them naked so that they fled from the house!

Can you see that? Can you imagine that as a YouTube video? Not good.

Spreading God's love is not about incantations, mimicry, or a formula. And reaching others is not about sharing on your own. True, joyful GO-ing is a team effort—done in the will of our Father, the power of the Holy Spirit, and the name of Jesus, and supplied from start to finish by the overflow of God's work in us! Our Father leads us. Jesus authorizes us. And the Spirit empowers us.

Paul stood in contrast to the foolish sons of Sceva.

- The only reason he was in Ephesus was because *God His Father had led him there.*
- The only reason he had authority was because *Jesus, the Son of God, had deputized him to speak in His name.*
- And the only reason Paul had power was because *he operated in the Holy Spirit.*

As a result, in Ephesus, "God was performing extraordinary miracles by the hands of Paul, so that handkerchiefs or aprons were even carried from his body to the sick, and the diseases left them and the evil spirits went out" (verses 11–12). Verses 17–20 tell us: "This became known to all, both Jews and Greeks, who lived in Ephesus; and fear fell upon them all and the name of the Lord Jesus was being magnified. Many also of those who had believed kept coming, confessing and disclosing their practices. . . . So the word of the Lord was growing mightily and prevailing."

Paul's team evangelism led to this citywide outbreak of the gospel, whereas the efforts of Sceva's sons led to empty results.

A VERY GOOD EXAMPLE

Who are your role models? Who do you look to as examples in the key areas of your life? What kind of impact does each of those people have on you in those areas?

So much of our success *and confidence* depends on the examples we are following.

Since this is true, let's follow Jesus as our example. He is the one to infuse confidence in us as we GO.

Luke 4:40–44 reports,

> While the sun was setting, all those who had any who were sick with various diseases brought them to Him; and laying His hands on each one of them, He was healing them. Demons also were coming out of many, shouting, "You are the Son of God!" But rebuking them, He would not allow them to speak, because they knew Him to be the Christ.
>
> When day came, Jesus left and went to a secluded place; and the crowds were searching for Him, and came to Him and tried to keep Him from going away from them. But He said to them, "I must preach the kingdom of God to the other cities also, for I was sent for this purpose."
>
> So He kept on preaching in the synagogues of Judea.

To say that Jesus was successful is an understatement. Whether He was casting out demons, healing the sick, or preaching the gospel, Jesus excelled. Let's make sure we understand what was behind His work, what made Him so successful.

Jesus employed Trinitarian GO-ing. He did not exorcise, heal, or preach on His own. He did so in the will of His Father, in the power of the Holy Spirit, and in the authority of His name. Watch this...

John the Baptist was the forerunner, the advance messenger, of Jesus. He came preaching a baptism of repentance of sins. Many people in Israel flocked to him as he ministered in the area of the Jordan River. The Jews wondered if he was actually the chosen one of God. John told them he was not, that the One to come was greater than him.

John was, of course, referring to Jesus.

Luke 3:21–22 tells of the day when Jesus came to John and submitted Himself to baptism: "Now when all the people were baptized, Jesus was also baptized, and while He was praying, heaven was opened, and the Holy Spirit descended upon Him in bodily form like a dove, and a voice came out of heaven, 'You are My beloved Son, in You I am well-pleased.'"

Here is Trinitarian affirmation—Jesus, the Son of God, affirmed and approved by God the Father and filled by God the Spirit. Luke 4:1 records Jesus' next steps: "Jesus, full of the Holy Spirit, returned from the Jordan and was led around by the Spirit in the wilderness for forty days, being tempted by the devil." And verses 14–15 of that chapter tell us, "Jesus returned [from the wilderness] to Galilee in the power of the Spirit, and news about

Him spread through all the surrounding district. And He began teaching in their synagogues and was praised by all."

To abundantly and joyfully share your salvation story, you must look to Jesus' model. He was not alone. He did not walk alone. And He did not work alone. Jesus was successful because He lived in the *faithfulness* of His Father, in the *fullness* of who He was as God's Son, and in the *power* of the Holy Spirit.

Trinitarian GO-ing is a game changer. It's the difference between playing one-on-five in basketball and being on Michael Jordan's team. Being teamed up with the Father, Son, and Holy Spirit, knowing that they are working in and through you as you speak to others about Jesus, is an enormous benefit.

FATHER

Brian screamed at his younger brother, Roger: "What do you think you're doing? You're not allowed to be in here! If you don't get out right now, I'm going to knock you out!"

Without batting an eye, Roger calmly turned to Brian and said, "Dad said I could."

Brian's anger instantly drained from his body. He was silenced.

There is real confidence when you are in the will of Dad!

In *BE: The Way of Rest*, I clarified the roles of the Father, Son, and Holy Spirit in our daily lives. One of the specific roles of our Father is to faithfully direct us. He has a will for each of us. In the garden of Gethsemane, Jesus the Son prayed to His Father, "Not My will, but Yours be done."[1] And in Matthew 6:10, He

---

[1] Luke 22:42.

taught us to ask of our Father, "Your kingdom come. Your will be done."

Pastor R. C. Sproul wrote, "Pursuing knowledge of the will of God is not an abstract science designed to titillate the intellect or to convey the kind of knowledge that 'puffs up' but fails to edify. An understanding of the will of God is desperately important for every Christian seeking to live a life that is pleasing to his or her Creator. It is a very practical thing for us to know what God wants for our lives."[2]

As Christians, we surrender our wills, our plans, to our Father, knowing that He is faithful to guide us to His will and plans. Through submission, we have the confidence of knowing that wherever we are, and whatever we're doing in obedience, God our Father has lovingly directed us to this circumstance. Like Roger, we can be at peace that Dad said we could!

And, because our Father is the God of all creation, there's nowhere we can go, and no person we can speak to, that is outside of His jurisdiction. You can operate in His holy will in a New York City boardroom; the living room of a friend in Lincoln, Nebraska; a client site in Bend, Oregon; a road in Perth, Australia; an alley in Calcutta, India; or anywhere else on Planet Earth. If you're in His will, then our Father, the Creator of all, is faithfully leading you.

SON

When we evangelize, not only are we speaking in the will of our Father, but we are declaring the name of Jesus.

---

[2] R. C. Sproul, *Can I Know God's Will?*, The Crucial Questions Series, vol. 4 (Lake Mary, FL: Reformation Trust Publishing, 2009), 29.

In Matthew 10 and Luke 10, Jesus sent out His disciples on their own for the first time. In sending them, Jesus gave them authority to preach the gospel, heal the sick, and cast out demons. He deputized them with His authority. They were constantly saying . . .

"We come in the name of Jesus."

"In the name of Jesus be healed."

"In the name of Jesus be freed."

"In the name of Jesus be saved."

A junior-level employee is tasked by the president of the company to collect information from various mid- and senior-level employees. When the junior-level employee approaches her superiors, they initially scoff at her request. Yet she isn't flustered or frustrated; she is unfazed. All she has to say is, "The president sent me," and instantly the responses of her superiors change.

According to the Population Reference Bureau, a nonprofit organization whose mission is to collect statistics that inform and shape healthy populations, an estimated total of 108 billion humans have lived on earth. By 2050, the Bureau estimates the number will climb to 113 billion.[3] I have no idea how they calculate it, but that's an enormous amount of people!

Scripture says that only God the Father knows the time when Jesus will return. When He determines the moment, the Father will once again say to the Son, "It is time," and Jesus will return. Imagine Jesus as He gathers Himself. What is the expression on His face as He presses His hands on the armrests of His throne to

---

[3] Toshiko Kaneda and Carl Haub, "How Many People Have Ever Lived on Earth?" Population Reference Bureau, January 23, 2020, https://www.prb.org/howmanypeoplehaveeverlivedonearth/.

lift His body to a standing position? What is happening in heaven as the Son of God takes His first steps toward His glorious return to earth? I can imagine a holy silence falling upon all who witness this breathtaking moment.

Many events will take place when Jesus returns. One of them is recorded in Philippians 2: "God highly exalted Him, and bestowed on Him the name which is above every name, so that at the name of Jesus every knee will bow, of those who are in heaven and on earth and under the earth, and every tongue will confess that Jesus Christ is Lord, to the glory of God the Father" (verses 9–11).

Here is the scene. Let's say that the Father sends Jesus back in 2050, and the PRB numbers are accurate—113 billion people have been born up to this time. Additionally, some unknown number of humans have died or have been killed in the womb. For the sake of this exercise, let's say that is an additional 1 billion people. At some point, 114 billion people from all of human history will stand before Jesus. At some point, 114 billion people will kneel before Jesus. At some point, 114 billion people will confess that Jesus Christ is Lord.

There is absolute power in the name of Jesus!

Men possessed by Satan's demons fell at Jesus' feet, begging Him for mercy. Sickness and disease fled from His touch. Religious and political leaders were stumped at His words. Even death bowed down before Him.

Be present in the truth that you GO in the name of Jesus. Rest in Him, His name, and the authority that is yours by grace. Do not waver. You can speak boldly in the overflow of the One to whom *every* knee will bow.

SPIRIT

We've previously explored the presence and power of the Holy Spirit in the ministry of Jesus. Understanding the Spirit's role is critical.

For a long time after becoming a Christian, I believed that Jesus succeeded simply because He was God the Son. I knew He was baptized in the Spirit by John, but I had no idea of the role the Spirit played. Somewhere along the way, I read Gerald Hawthorne's *The Presence and the Power: The Significance of the Holy Spirit in the Life and Ministry of Jesus*,[4] and my eyes were opened. What Jesus truly modeled for us was a life perfectly submitted to the Holy Spirit. Jesus' life was Spirit life.

Consider the benefits we receive from the Holy Spirit just in evangelism:

- "When they hand you over, do not worry about how or what you are to say; for it will be given you in that hour what you are to say. For it is not you who speak, but it is the Spirit of your Father who speaks in you."[5]
- [Jesus said,] "You will receive power when the Holy Spirit has come upon you; and you shall be My witnesses both in Jerusalem, and in all Judea and Samaria, and even to the remotest part of the earth."[6]
- "Stephen, full of grace and power, was performing great wonders and signs among the people. But some men from what was called the Synagogue of the Freedmen,

---

[4] Gerald Hawthorne, *The Presence and the Power: The Significance of the Holy Spirit in the Life and Ministry of Jesus* (Eugene, OR: Wipf and Stock, 2003).
[5] Matthew 10:19–20.
[6] Acts 1:8.

including both Cyrenians and Alexandrians, and some from Cilicia and Asia, rose up and argued with Stephen. But they were unable to cope with the wisdom and the Spirit with which he was speaking."[7]

- "Now there were at Antioch, in the church that was there, prophets and teachers: Barnabas, and Simeon . . . , and Lucius of Cyrene, and Manaen . . . , and Saul. While they were ministering to the Lord and fasting, the Holy Spirit said, 'Set apart for Me Barnabas and Saul for the work to which I have called them.' Then, when they had fasted and prayed and laid their hands on them, they sent them away. So, being sent out by the Holy Spirit, they went down to Seleucia and from there they sailed to Cyprus."[8]

- "[Paul and Timothy] passed through the Phrygian and Galatian region, having been forbidden by the Holy Spirit to speak the word in Asia; and after they came to Mysia, they were trying to go into Bithynia, and the Spirit of Jesus did not permit them; and passing by Mysia, they came down to Troas. A vision appeared to Paul in the night: a man of Macedonia was standing and appealing to him, and saying, 'Come over to Macedonia and help us.' When he had seen the vision, immediately we sought to go into Macedonia, concluding that God had called us to preach the gospel to them."[9]

---

[7] Acts 6:8–10.
[8] Acts 13:1–4.
[9] Acts 16:6–10.

You must see that evangelism is a supernatural, organic work empowered and led by the Holy Spirit. Sharing Jesus is not you merely mustering strength, overcoming fears, finding people, and saying the right things on your own. That vision must be done away with. Reaching people is done in the fluid rhythms of the Holy Spirit.

As you grow in intimacy with Him and become more comfortable with His leading, He will send you to people. He will give you visions. He will give you words. He will give you power to confront whatever or whomever you face. And, He will enable you to persevere as you need to.

We go and share according to the will of God the Father, in the name of Jesus, in the anointing of the Holy Spirit. This is not golf. This is not you being trained and sent out onto the course of life by yourself to do the best you can. This is you on God's mission, with God's presence to reach the people God has given you to reach.

Golf GO-ing is daunting.

Trinitarian GO-ing is exhilarating!

DOES IT REALLY MATTER?

Sometimes there is confusion about how God's sovereignty intersects with our work. People wonder: But isn't God sovereign? Doesn't He already know who will say yes and who will say no? Won't He reach people regardless? What's the point of me GO-ing?

If this is wrongly understood, Christians can easily convince themselves that they don't need to go and share. If rightly understood, Christians will joyfully go forth and look for opportunities to share.

So how does all of this work?

I was in the room, front and center, when my son and daughter were born. There was no way I was going to miss a moment of either of their births. As they came into the world, I was stunned. And then I cried. Both times. I was in awe that, in partnership with my wife, someone like me could be involved in *creating* life. As I look at my son and daughter today, I am in awe that each of them is 50 percent me!

But I know that my kids are not just the coming together of Brooke's and my DNA. They are the result of God our Father's providential work that He blessed us to participate in.

God could have established creation in such a way that He just "materialized" people, with men and women having no role at all. He could have established creation so that He simply "deposited" an infant in the womb of a woman or a man (if God had chosen to give a womb to males). But, in His divine and perfect wisdom, God created men and women distinctly, designing us and enabling us to participate with Him in the wonders of creating life. What an astounding miracle!

Likewise, God our Father has enabled us to participate in the wonders of creating new life in Him through sharing the gospel. We have the awe-inspiring privilege of passing along the Good News by which a person may be birthed into God's kingdom, adopted into His family, raised from death to life, saved from eternal condemnation, and delivered to eternal restoration.

J. I. Packer wrote, "While we must always remember that it is our responsibility to proclaim salvation, we must never forget that it is God who saves. It is God who brings men and women under the sound of the Gospel, and it is God who brings them to faith in Christ. Our evangelistic work is the instrument that He uses for this purpose, but the power that saves is not in the instrument: it is in the hand of the One who uses the instrument."[10]

Let us stand in awe with the apostle Paul at being entrusted with the gospel: "We have this treasure in earthen vessels, so that the surpassing greatness of the power will be of God and not from ourselves."[11]

Let us rebuke the lie that our evangelistic efforts are irrelevant "since God knows who is going to receive Him anyway."

Or that we can leave the work to someone else, as if our story doesn't matter.

Or that we ever go it alone.

Let us step into the full joy of striving together through Trinitarian evangelism to reach every person who has not heard of Jesus until the day our Father calls us home.

> *Now the God of peace, who brought up from the*
> *dead the great Shepherd of the sheep through the blood of*
> *the eternal covenant, even Jesus our Lord, equip*
> *you in every good thing to do His will, working in us*
> *that which is pleasing in His sight, through Jesus Christ,*
> *to whom be the glory forever and ever. Amen.*
> Hebrews 13:20–21

---

[10] J. I. Packer, *Evangelism and the Sovereignty of God* (Downers Grove, Illinois: InterVarsity Press, 1961), 27.
[11] 2 Corinthians 4:7.

NO COLD CALLS

A "cold call" is when a salesperson reaches out to a potential client for the first time. The assumption is that the potential client has never heard of the salesperson's company, product, or service. The caller has to start from the beginning.

In Trinitarian GO-ing, we make no cold calls.

We believe, because of the sacrifice of Jesus and the wonder of God in creation, that the Holy Spirit has already been working on the heart and mind of every person we will be sent to.

Paul affirmed this in Romans 1:18–20:

> For the wrath of God is revealed from heaven against all ungodliness and unrighteousness of men who suppress the truth in unrighteousness, because that which is known about God is evident within them; for God made it evident to them. For since the creation of the world His invisible attributes, His eternal power and divine nature, have been clearly seen, being understood through what has been made, so that they are without excuse.

God has written Himself on the heart of every person everywhere. As we are sent to speak, He has already been inviting that person to Himself. We are simply stepping into the flow of what He's been doing.

We also strongly believe that God the Father, Son, and Holy Spirit wants that person to be saved *far more* than we do. He is not just sending you—He has been moving in that individual's life from the day they were born. Nevertheless, even with all the divine wooing that occurs in the Spirit, through you and others, an individual still must choose to surrender. Sadly, not all do. There is no formula that guarantees their positive response.

Always, though, God is actively working to awaken people. Reflect on your own story and remember what He did in you. See the many ways our Father wooed you. Recall the people He sent. Likewise, God creatively, in customized ways, gives every person opportunity to say yes to abundant, eternal life through Jesus. God loves people—and He loves the people He sends you to. He sends *you* because He loves *them*! GO in the bold assurance of the all-star team you're on—Team Father, Son, and Holy Spirit—and share your story!

Chapter Work: Don't Golf

1. Write out your understanding of the role of the Father, Son, and Holy Spirit in personal evangelism.

   Father

   Son

   Holy Spirit

2. What about Trinitarian evangelism is most meaningful to you?

3. Many people can be deceived into believing that they do not have to share their story because if God wants to reach other people, He will get someone else to do it. Why is it important for you to be faithful to share with those our Father sends you to? What do you understand about the relationship between God's providence and your responsibility?

4. Effective flexing happens in the rhythm of the Spirit. What is one effective strategy you can use to remind yourself that the Holy Spirit is already actively working in any person with whom you are going to share?

6 Bait

Kris Culpepper is a professional fisherman who has won numerous Fishing League Worldwide Redfish Series tournaments, been featured in magazines, and appeared in fishing shows on television. Because Jesus offered to make His first four disciples, who were fishermen, into *fishers of men*, I thought it would be interesting to talk to a professional fisherman about his expertise.

I wanted to ask Kris about bait in particular. How important is what you put on your hook to catching fish? Does it really matter? And, how do you know what bait to use?

Here are some excellent quotes from our conversation that are meaningful for us as we go to share the love of Jesus with others:

- Fishing takes a lot of effort. The exciting and rewarding part is when you catch something.
- Catching fish is about making adjustments. If what you're using isn't working, you have to change it up.

- Understanding what bait is in season is extremely important for catching fish.
- Every fish feeds on different bait at different times.

Kris also told me that in the winter, speckled trout will only eat once every one to two days because they're trying to conserve energy. When they feed, they typically seek larger food like mullet. However, in the spring, when the water is warmer, speckled trout prefer smaller food like shrimp and minnows.

I find this fascinating for many reasons. First, because of the incredible variety of God's creation. The wonders of His work in nature never cease to amaze. Second, it's fascinating to me because of the parallels with Jesus' work and training in fishing for souls.

Jesus regularly made "adjustments," understanding that "every fish [person] feeds on different bait at different times." It was exciting and rewarding for Him, too, when He caught something (gained a new disciple). Jesus loved when people heard His words and followed Him!

As we will see in this chapter, He rarely used the same approach, or even the same wording. He tuned in to the individual or individuals He was talking to and what they needed to hear. Being flexible in this way is always the go-to approach. But as you advance in sharing God's love, you'll want to learn different approaches so that you can flex even better. Remember, Jesus is making you into a fisher of men. He will guide you to become more effective. He will teach you how to more clearly discern the leading of the Holy Spirit and be increasingly aware of the needs of the one with whom you are sharing.

Consider the following examples and the different ways in which He or His disciples shared the gospel. We can learn the same approaches.

"COME AND SEE" GOSPEL

In two instances at the beginning of Jesus' ministry, His disciples told others to "come and see" Jesus. Andrew, the brother of Peter, had already seen Jesus and surrendered. John 1:41–42 says that Andrew promptly sought out his own brother Peter (also called Simon) and said to him, "We have found the Messiah," and he brought him to Jesus so that Simon could see for himself. The next day, after Jesus invited Philip to begin following Him, Philip found Nathanael and said to him, "Come and see" (verse 46). Once Jesus had spoken to both Peter and Nathanael, the men accepted His invitation and were saved.

At heart, we are saying, "Come and see!" to nonbelievers anytime we invite them to church, share a Christian book with them, or send them a link to a sermon or other message about Jesus: "My favorite author just did a powerful podcast about what happens when we die. I learned a great deal that I think you would benefit from hearing. Take a listen!"

STRAIGHTFORWARD GOSPEL

In Jesus' first recorded sermon in Mark 1:15, He said, "The time is fulfilled, and the kingdom of God is at hand; repent and believe in the gospel." Now that's a straightforward gospel presentation! Right to the point!

As crowds began to press in on Him, Jesus regularly invoked

His dedication to spreading the gospel far and wide: "I must preach the kingdom of God to the other cities also, for I was sent for this purpose."[1]

Jesus used these key elements in His first sermon:

- *Timing.* "The time is fulfilled." How did Jesus know the time was fulfilled? Because our Father told Him it was. In straightforward gospel sharing, we also ought to be sensitive to our Father's timing.
- *Presence.* "The kingdom of God is at hand." God is at work in the world. He is available and accessible.
- *Accountability.* "Repent." Each person has to take responsibility for their sin. To repent means to turn around and go in the opposite direction. Through repentance, a person confesses they have lived apart from God and have come to a place where they are ready to start walking with God.
- *Receptivity.* "Believe in the gospel." To receive the gospel is to accept that Jesus died on the cross for the forgiveness of one's sins, to begin a new relationship with Him where He is Lord and Savior, to be adopted into the family of God, and to be filled with the Holy Spirit.

Many Christians have been trained in straightforward gospel presentation by learning what is called "the Romans Road." This

---

[1] Luke 4:43.

is a simple, five-step summary of Paul's letter to the church in ancient Rome:

1) We are all sinners by nature and by choice (Romans 3:23).
2) We receive eternal life as a free gift (6:23).
3) God demonstrated His love for us, His enemies (5:8).
4) We must trust and surrender to Jesus as Lord (10:9-10).
5) Our assurance of salvation is through Jesus (10:13).

Many variations of a straightforward gospel presentation exist. You may use the *Four Spiritual Laws*[2] by Campus Crusade for Christ (renamed Cru) founder Bill Bright. I've also seen teenagers have great success using an EvangeCube on the foreign mission field. With any of these methods, make sure you master your presentation so that it comes across naturally.

SPECIFIC-ISSUES GOSPEL

I think this was Jesus' favorite method. He loved to identify specific issues in potential followers. With pinpoint accuracy, Jesus got at the heart of what was keeping the person in front of Him from accepting His love.

- Nicodemus was trapped in religion. Jesus told him religion was his barrier. Consequently, Nicodemus needed to be born again.[3]

---

[2] The original edition is available on a limited basis. Cru has updated the original booklet and changed the name to *Would You Like to Know God Personally?*
[3] John 3:1–21.

- The woman at the well was trapped in immorality, gender issues, cultural prejudice, and worship confusion. Jesus told her she could taste of His living water in spite of these.[4]
- The rich young ruler was trapped in his affluence. Jesus told him if he would sell all his possessions and give them to the poor, he could have treasure in heaven.[5]
- Zaccheus was trapped in greed and deceitful tax schemes. Jesus simply noticed Zaccheus and spoke the man's name, and this tax collector repented of his financial sin.[6]

In each of these instances, Jesus never used the same wording. He saw into the person in front of Him and treated each individual's situation differently. He didn't offer a one-size-fits-all response.

Now, I am not Jesus. I don't have His precise insight into people. I can't instantly discern their stories. However, I can ask some simple questions to get to know the person I'm talking to. By listening to their stories, their obstacles to faith will become readily apparent. One woman I know of idolized her children. One man I met idolized his wife and felt he couldn't make a decision for the Lord for fear of what it would do to his marriage. Another person I know was addicted to work. Another individual was under the thumb of their parents and afraid of Mom and Dad's judgment.

There may be times when the Holy Spirit will give us insight

---

[4] John 4:1–26.
[5] Luke 18:18–27.
[6] Luke 19:1–10.

into people that we could not have on our own. Remember, God the Father is intimately acquainted with the one you're speaking to. He wants them saved more than you do. And His Spirit is at work today, speaking God's Word into people's hearts and lives. We must cultivate the ability to listen not only to each individual but to the Holy Spirit, to discern what He's whispering to us in these moments. He knows all about this person, and He often gives us wisdom and insight into what they need and how to approach them.

The Holy Spirit also works by gifting some people to know details about others without the person having ever said so, like we see in Jesus. We want to be open to what the Holy Spirit says to us. If you're unsure if what you have is from the Spirit, you can begin by saying, "I'm not sure if this is accurate, but I sense the Lord showing me that you . . ." We walk and work in grace. Our Father loves that you are seeking Him, learning to listen to His Spirit, and courageous enough to speak. Give the person the opportunity to affirm or deny what you share, and let the conversation flow from there.

Whether you glean an issue by asking questions or by the Spirit's revelation, please be careful when speaking. Be full of love and grace. Having one's issues pointed out is hard for most people. Be empathetic—you have plenty of issues you battle yourself. If the person walks away, make sure they know you are always available when they are ready to talk.

THE SIGNS AND WONDERS GOSPEL

Jesus had a complicated relationship with signs and wonders. By "signs and wonders," I mean performing miracles (such as

Jesus feeding the 5,000 in John 6:1–14), healing the sick (for example, Luke 5:12–26), and casting out demons (as we see in Luke 8:26–39).[7] Signs and wonders were always meant to lead people to faith; Jesus never used them for the sake of showing off or manipulating people. He only performed miracles as a means of opening hearts to receive His love.

And therein lies the nature of the complication. Signs were often inadequate for saving souls, even though people wanted to see them all the time.

In John 4:46–54, Jesus was in Cana, a city in Galilee, when a royal official came to Him and asked Him to heal his son who was near death in the neighboring city of Capernaum. Jesus replied, "Unless you people see signs and wonders, you simply will not believe" (verse 48).

After performing the incredible miracle of feeding more than 5,000[8] people in John 6, Jesus said to the crowd, "Truly, truly, I say to you, you seek Me, not because you saw signs, but because you ate of the loaves and were filled. Do not work for the food which perishes, but for the food which endures to eternal life, which the Son of Man will give to you, for on Him the Father, God, has set His seal" (verses 26–27).

Finally, in an incredible story in Luke 17, Jesus crossed paths with ten men who were suffering from the horrific disease of leprosy. Verses 11–19 tell how Jesus healed all ten men. They were

---

[7] This third example is a great story of Jesus delivering a man from demonic possession who then goes to his hometown and tells everyone his story. Jesus' signs and wonders led to a man flexing his story power!

[8] Because in ancient writings only men were counted, the actual number fed is more than 10,000.

freed from an incurable disease. Yet of the ten, only one came back to thank Jesus. One! These men had experienced the miracle of healing directly—they weren't just bystanders to someone else's miracle. You can hear the frustration and sadness in Jesus' reply: "Were there not ten cleansed? But the nine—where are they? Was no one found who returned to give glory to God, except this foreigner? And He said to [the one who returned to thank Him], 'Stand up and go; your faith has made you well'" (verses 17–19).

Jesus' earthly ministry showed the limited effectiveness of signs and wonders.

This is very confusing to me. As one who loves to see people be saved, and as one who loves to read the book of Acts where signs and wonders are happening on nearly every page,[9] I have often wondered why miracles are not more prevalent in my life. Why would God not empower His people with a greater capacity for signs and wonders?

But Scripture shows that while these supernatural acts can be useful, they only rarely produce genuine Christ followers. Nevertheless, the Holy Spirit is at work today, healing the sick and casting out demons for the purpose of opening hearts to faith. I have witnessed healings. I have cast out demons. More important than any sign or miracle, I have led people into a loving relationship with the Father, Son, and Holy Spirit.

---

[9] Acts, the account of the Holy Spirit expanding the gospel from Jerusalem to Rome, reads almost like a diary from the days of the wild American frontier. In report after report, we read of the Spirit moving through Jesus' disciples as they engaged with people in new geographies to spread the gospel. In one example, one of Jesus' original twelve disciples, Philip, was in Samaria preaching the gospel. Acts 8:7–8 says, "In the case of many who had unclean spirits, they were coming out of them shouting with a loud voice; and many who had been paralyzed and lame were healed. So there was much rejoicing in that city."

One important note about signs and wonders. Every biblical example of these incredible works happens as the person performing them is actively engaged in reaching people. Jesus and His disciples were faithful to GO as the Spirit led them. They were equipped with these gifts as they were sent. Great power is available for the one who is willing to GO. The power of God in signs and wonders is richly present on the foreign mission field as we give ourselves to becoming fishers of men for Jesus.

THE RELATIONSHIP GOSPEL

Wayne Hastings, a veteran in Christian publishing, tells a story about sharing Jesus' love by building relationships:

> My friend Ken [not his real name] became very disappointed in his home church. As a conscientious objector to the Vietnam War, he felt the church didn't help him. Consequently, Ken fled to Canada and returned home only when President Jimmy Carter declared amnesty.
>
> Soon after his return to the US, Ken and I began playing racquetball and later tennis at least twice a week. I was fairly new to the faith, and Ken and I competed hard with each other, talking about a myriad of things. He shared his story with me, and I shared my story with him, but he was very skeptical of the church and Christianity. I didn't push things—I enjoyed our time together, treasured our friendship, and kept sharing pieces of my story.
>
> One day, about two years after we began our regular competitive outings, Ken told me he had gone to church. I

must have looked shocked because Ken joked, "Well, it's your fault!" He later went on to tell me that he saw that my life was different. He admired my strong family and faith, and he'd become convinced that all the misgivings he'd once had about Christians and the church were due to his limited knowledge. "You're so different," he said. "You never preached to me; you just accepted me and loved me as a friend."

What I realized was that my life was a witness. If I had approached Ken with a hard-and-fast evangelism approach, he would have run away and I would've missed out on a wonderful friend—and lots of tennis. My story and my life (with all its weaknesses) was witness enough for Ken.[10]

What Wayne describes is often called *relational*, or *lifestyle*, *evangelism*. Jesus prescribed this in the Sermon on the Mount, when He said, "Let your light shine before men in such a way that they may see your good works, and glorify your Father who is in heaven."[11] Through relationships, people get to see the difference Jesus makes in us. They're able to see the good works that He leads us to do that we would not have done otherwise. The light of Jesus in us opens up the nonbeliever to receive Christ and be saved.

Jesus even used relational evangelism while He was hanging on the cross. Luke 23 records that one of the criminals who was being crucified alongside Jesus hurled insults at Him. The second criminal rebuked the first, saying about Jesus, "This man has done nothing wrong" (verse 41). Then he said to Jesus, "Remember me

---

[10] Personal correspondence with author, May 2020.
[11] Matthew 5:16.

when You come in Your kingdom!" (verse 42). Ever the missionary, even dying on the cross, Jesus replied, "Truly I say to you, today you shall be with Me in Paradise" (verse 43).

What made this man finally turn his life over to Jesus? Based on the way he rebuked his fellow criminal, it seems he had known of Jesus from before. Why now?

I believe it's because of what he heard Jesus say when their crosses were first raised into place. Earlier, in Luke 23:34, right after Jesus and the two criminals were hung on crosses by Roman centurions, Jesus said, "Father, forgive them; for they do not know what they are doing." The repentant criminal heard that and was shocked. What kind of man prays that God would forgive the ones who are guilty of his unjust murder? What kind of man is this?

The light of Jesus shone bright. The repentant criminal beheld Christ's good works, confessed his sinfulness, glorified God in heaven, and was saved!

We see the same scenario with Stephen, one of the first deacons of the church at Jerusalem. Brought before the Jewish Council in Acts 6, Stephen gives a robust defense of his faith, telling his Jesus story in the next chapter. The Jews were so agitated by his words that they drove Stephen out of the chambers and stoned him to death. As he fell to his knees, Stephen cried out, "Lord, do not hold this sin against them!" (Acts 7:60). The next verse, Acts 8:1, tells us, "Saul was in hearty agreement with putting him to death." Saul, who would soon be converted by Jesus as he traveled from Jerusalem to Damascus, had a front-row seat to the Jesus-difference in Stephen's life.

I wonder how many times in his later missionary career Paul thought about Stephen.

I wonder what the reunion looked like when Paul went to the great banqueting feast in heaven and saw Stephen for the first time.

We practice relational evangelism anytime we model the life of Jesus to others. Those who do not believe in Him can see and hear what we do and say, and we trust that they will be drawn in by the light in us. Consider these examples:

- Like Jesus, we bless our enemies and do not curse them.
- We meet the physical needs of our neighbors, friends, and family.
- We offer prayer as comfort and encouragement.
- We use words of kindness and grace.
- We model internal rest that comes from trusting in God's faithfulness.
- We give sound words of wisdom at appropriate times.
- We no longer practice sin like we used to.[12]

The apostle Paul encouraged the believers in Galatia, "Let us not lose heart in doing good, for in due time we will reap if we do not grow weary. So then, while we have opportunity, let us do good to all people, and especially to those who are of the household of the faith."[13] As we intentionally build relationships with others, people gain a front-row seat to the effect of an authentic relationship

---

[12] Peter wrote in 1 Peter 4:1–5 that those with whom we used to sin see a difference in us as we walk away from our old lifestyles. I can certainly testify to the power a changed life can have on those I once partied with.
[13] Galatians 6:9–10.

with Jesus. In a culture like America's, where many people have been damaged by the church and/or Christians, relational evangelism can be a great way to open people's hearts to the love of Christ.

Relational evangelism can take a long time—sometimes a lifetime. Don't give up. Regularly connect with your friends and family and co-workers without feeling pressured to share the gospel. If the Holy Spirit tells you to speak, speak. If He does not, you can delight in His divine strategy to perhaps share with them further down the road or to reach other hearts as the light of Christ shines in you.

But let me also caution you not to hide behind relational evangelism. "I don't like telling people about Jesus—I just like to live and let them see Jesus in me" is a dangerous attitude that people use to justify not sharing the gospel. No matter who we're with, we just want to be available to the Lord as He leads.

DEBATE GOSPEL

I've frequently heard Christians speak against debating with others about Christianity, invoking some form of the statement "Whatever you argue someone into, they can be argued out of." I think that's an unfortunate sentiment. What I hope they mean is, you can't yell someone into the kingdom of God. Like a husband and wife who have hit a rough patch and heatedly try to convince the other of their correctness, an argument with a nonbeliever that devolves into yelling is pointless.

However, a robust debate can be very useful in sharing Christ's love. Jesus debated the religious leaders of His day on various issues including His identity, the Sabbath, tithing, ceremonial washing, and marriage-divorce-remarriage. After our Lord's crucifixion, Joseph of Arimathea, who was a prominent religious leader, asked for the body of Jesus. We are told that at some point, Joseph had become a follower of Christ, receiving Jesus' love and salvation. Could he have been opened to faith in part by being on hand as Jesus engaged in debates?

Scripture says Paul often debated others: "*According to Paul's custom*, he went to them, and for three Sabbaths reasoned with them from the Scriptures, explaining and giving evidence that the Christ had to suffer and rise again from the dead, and saying, 'This Jesus whom I am proclaiming to you is the Christ.' And some of them were persuaded."[14]

The Greek verb translated "reasoned with" (*dialegomai*) denotes "discoursed, argued, discussed." That Paul was debating or arguing is seen in the diametric responses of those who listened to his words: some people were persuaded and others reacted violently. Debating was an effective tool for Paul. Through these exchanges, he saw many people receive the love of Jesus.

One of Paul's techniques was to urge his listeners to reason their way through a verse. In this way, he initiated a discussion. He opened a dialogue that gave him more knowledge about the other person's views. Then he could explain from his story and help them understand the good news of the gospel. We can do the same thing, asking a person to think about what a verse says, what it implies, and what it communicates about Jesus—listening all the while to gain further understanding about them.

---

[14] Acts 17:2–4.

Debating can be treacherous and hurtful to others. Engaging in debate can be a source of pride. So we must exercise caution. We aren't debating to win an argument and prove our intellectual superiority or to shame anyone. If we debate, we do so with love, to see others come to faith.

Also, engaging in debate can be a waste of time if the ones we're talking to have no desire to hear. Jesus warned, "Do not throw your pearls before swine, or they will trample them under their feet, and turn and tear you to pieces."[15] Yikes! The picture of being torn to pieces by swine is startling!

Engaging in debate can also be dangerous when we are scripturally ignorant or uninformed on an issue. As a rule of thumb, if you don't know the consistent teaching of Scripture on a subject from the Old Testament to the New, then you aren't ready to debate it. Jesus and Paul studied; they didn't simply show up with a couple of Bible verses out of context and start running their mouths. They did their homework.

Let's remember that our work to reach people is done only in rhythm with the Father, Son, and Holy Spirit. If God our Father is leading you to debate, then debate in the love of Jesus and the Holy Spirit. Be careful that you don't go looking for fights. Pastor Jon Courson recommends this:

> As seen so beautifully in the ministry of Paul, the key to opening the Scriptures is always to look for, talk about, and focus on the Person of Jesus Christ. Whether sharing with children,

---

[15] Matthew 7:6.

talking to a neighbor, or teaching a Bible study—the key to opening . . . hearts is to look not for principles of parenting or methods of marital communication, but for Jesus Christ. Our faith is not in a philosophy, not in principles, but in a Person. You will be a wonderful Bible student and an excellent Bible teacher if you learn this simple lesson: talk about *Jesus*. Look for *Jesus*. *He* is the key to opening Scripture.[16]

No matter what "bait" we use as we "fish for souls," our passion is to see the one with whom we're sharing come to faith in Jesus and begin to walk in His fuller, richer life. Our goal is not to perform signs and wonders, win debates, or coldly point out others' specific needs. Our hearts should break for lost souls.

Ask Jesus to expand your skills and approaches to sharing His love. Try some of the additional ways we've discussed here. Learn from others who are consistently having those faith conversations. And do not grow weary in our Lord's work. You, too, can become a fisher of men.

---

[16] Jon Courson, *Jon Courson's Application Commentary: New Testament* (Nashville, TN: Thomas Nelson, 2003), 747.

Chapter Work:
Bait

Our Father effectively uses every personality type to share our Jesus-stories with others. In addition to flexing your story power, you can learn many other techniques from Scripture. Rate your comfort level in using the other techniques given to share the gospel.

_____ Come and see

_____ Straightforward

_____ Specific issues

_____ Signs and wonders

_____ Relationship

_____ Debate

1. If the Holy Spirit is prompting you to expand your skills in sharing, in which of the techniques above is He leading you to engage?

2. Whatever your preferred method of sharing Jesus is, what is one aspect of your method in which you can improve?

3. Spend time praying for the Holy Spirit to give you opportunities today to share Jesus with someone using one of the listed methods.

7   90/10

Kris Culpepper taught me another truism about fishing: 90 percent of the fish are in 10 percent of the water!

I never knew that!

The lesson is obvious—if you put your line in the 90 percent of water where there are no fish, there's a 100 percent chance you'll catch nothing. You can watch your carefully baited hook float through beautiful, fishless water, but you're wasting time by fishing in the wrong place. How much more successful would your fishing be if you had a guide—someone who could tell you where to cast your line and what kind of bait to use?

I have no problem confessing that I am a terrible fisherman. I caught a fish once and was trying to remove the hook when my catch made a "crying" noise! I freaked out and dropped the fish. (Obviously, I wasn't raised fishing!) So can you imagine how much my fishing would instantly transform if I had Kris Culpepper in my boat and I listened to him? All I'd have to do is listen and be faithful; then even someone like me could be successful!

SET FOR SUCCESS

In His incredible wisdom, God our Father gave us the ultimate fishing Guide. As we discussed in the chapter on Trinitarian sharing, the Holy Spirit is our fishing expert. He knows where the 10 percent water is. He knows the fish and where they are going to be. Our responsibility is to listen to Him. Learning to be still, hear His voice, and trust in His leading is essential to our success.

Unfortunately, even excellent listening doesn't always guarantee our success.

Recently, I prayed in the morning and asked the Lord to send me to someone I could share the gospel with. Most days I work on-site at Crosswalk, a ministry specializing in "re-entry discipleship"—they work inside and outside the prisons to provide men with a seamless path to re-enter society as strong followers of Jesus. The staff is all Christian. They graciously allow me to work in a back room where no one ever goes. So I asked the Lord to let me interact with someone about Jesus that day despite being in a back room in a place where I'm surrounded by Christians.

Midmorning, some guy walks into the room where I work. I think, *You have got to be kidding. This is awesome!* The man asks, "Mind if I look at the water heater? There's a leak in the building." I'm trying to figure out how to transition into a conversation about Jesus. There's no "leak in the water heater" verse in the Gospels for me to mention.

I take the repairman downstairs to show him other possible sources for the leak. On the way, I ask him his name. "Jesús," he says. *Excuse me? Crazy! I ask the Lord to give me someone I can talk to about Jesus, and He sends me Jesús!* But . . . my brain gets twisted and I fail to use that organic opportunity to share the gospel.

I leave him downstairs so I can regroup. My phone rings and I take the call. When I finish . . . Jesús is gone!

Argh!

We are all in the process of learning to become fishers of men. Therefore, we should all expect to make mistakes and miss opportunities. Fortunately, our Father is patient in working with us, and He delights in our heart's desire to see wayward people come home. So know that no matter where you are, our Father can use you to reach people.

Jerry Wiles is the North America Regional Director of the International Orality Network, a group of organizations launching church-planting movements by making God's Word available to oral communicators in culturally appropriate ways. He has been sharing Jesus with people for years. He told me, "Reaching people is not so much about methods and techniques as it is about prayer and following the leading of the Holy Spirit."

Jerry loves to tell the story from years ago of walking out of a hotel in Washington, D.C., on a rainy day. A woman was struggling to open her umbrella, and Jerry offered to help. Thus began a conversation in which Jerry felt led to ask her, "Have you been thinking more about the Lord lately?" The lady said yes, prompting Jerry to invite her to receive the love of Jesus!

A man named Brian was with Jerry at the time, watching the

whole event unfold. Years later, Brian told Jerry, "Ever since that day, I've been able to lead two to three people to the Lord a week. All I do is follow the leading of the Holy Spirit!"[1]

You may have a hard time seeing who you might ever be able to share with. Maybe most of "your people" are Christians. Maybe your family is already saved or has already heard "enough" from you. Maybe your company frowns on "religious" conversations. Maybe you are shy and the thought of approaching people scares you. There are plenty of scenarios that can cause us to doubt whether we could ever share with anyone. And if we were in it alone, some of those reservations might be legitimate. But we walk in the Holy Spirit of the living God. We walk with the One who is an expert at creating what are often called "divine appointments," completely impossible-to-plan intersections between two people, providentially orchestrated by God.

"All" Jesus was doing in John 4 at the well in Samaria was going to get water. There's nothing special about being thirsty; there's nothing special about wanting a cup of water. Unless the Holy Spirit is leading, that is. Then the simple act of getting water can be transformed into an eternally significant moment that leads to an entire city being saved.

That is the power of the Holy Spirit.

Our work is not to find people. Our work is to pray for God to use and create appointments for us. Then we rest in the Holy Spirit and follow where He leads.

---

[1] Personal conversation with the author on July 21, 2020.

SPIRIT-LED

Philip and Peter were coming off a successful mission trip to Samaria. The Holy Spirit had moved, and many were saved. Upon the pair's return to Jerusalem, an angel of the Lord spoke to Philip and directed him to the road to Gaza, a city fifty miles southwest of Jerusalem. Once he was on that road, Philip saw an Ethiopian eunuch—a member of the royal court of Candace, queen of Ethiopia—sitting in a chariot.

Who was Philip to speak to such an esteemed man? What did a blue-collar guy like Philip have to offer a member of a royal court? Looking at the circumstances through natural eyes, the scene seems odd. Here's what happened according to Acts 8: "Then the Spirit said to Philip, 'Go up and join this chariot.' Philip ran up and heard him reading Isaiah the prophet" (verses 29–30).

Pause.

Philip had no idea who this man was, and he had no idea what was going on in this man's life. From a distance, Philip couldn't see that the man was reading Scripture. The only thing Jesus' disciple knew was that the Holy Spirit told him to go. So he went.

Philip asked the eunuch, "Do you understand what you are reading?" (verse 30).

Notice that Philip commented on something the man was doing. He didn't walk up to him and start in with his gospel story. He observed that the Ethiopian was reading, and he asked him about it. How natural is it for you to notice and inquire about what someone is doing?

The eunuch replied that, in fact, he could not understand it and needed help. And he invited Philip to sit with him in his chariot and explain the prophet Isaiah's words (verses 31–35).

Philip couldn't have planned this. He never would have imagined this scenario. All Philip had to do was be faithful to the Holy Spirit and be willing to have a conversation.

Philip didn't get distracted by other issues either. He didn't bring up Ethiopian politics or the latest gossip about the queen. He used the Spirit-created opportunity to connect Isaiah and Jesus, showing how what the man was reading was fulfilled in Jesus.

The Ethiopian surrendered his life to the Lord! Then, seeing a body of water a little farther down the road, the eunuch asked Philip to baptize him. After this, the two men went their separate ways and never saw each other again (verses 36–39).

Now watch this. Ethiopian Christians in the year 2021 trace their roots back to this man! Two thousand years later, Ethiopians who walk with Jesus see their beginnings in this story—all because Philip followed the leading of the Holy Spirit, his fishing Guide.

As you open yourself to the leading of the Holy Spirit, missionary that you are, you will notice yourself interacting with more and more people one-on-one: a server at a restaurant, your neighbors, someone at the grocery store, co-workers, even the plumber! People who need Jesus are all around you.

The Holy Spirit seems to especially love using airplanes to create divine appointments. Traveling by plane provides a unique setting: you're seated next to someone for hours in a confined space with little else to do. How many times have you heard stories of God using a flight as an opportunity to reach someone He loves?

These kinds of interactions are what I call "working in your highways and byways." *Highways and byways* is just a way of describing your normal comings and goings. This isn't a night of door-to-door evangelism or going on a foreign mission trip. This is just living your life, energized by the Holy Spirit as a missionary. The places we frequent every day become our mission field—the park, restaurants, the grocery store, the gym . . . wherever we go. Not every trip to the store or the coffee shop will turn into a fifteen-minute gospel conversation. But some do. We just want to be open to the Spirit so that we can reach those He places in our path.

Of course, stepping into these opportunities requires our ability to notice the people around us.

THE MINISTRY OF NOTICING

Jesus paused in the middle of His missionary work one day. After He spent time preaching, healing, and casting out demons, I imagine He took a deep breath. Lifted His head. And looked at all the people, taking each one of them into His sight. He saw the entirety of each person—not just their faces, stature, and clothes. He saw through to the condition of their souls. He saw their pain, their fatigue, their strivings and dreams. He saw their brokenness.

This is why He came.

People.

And they are everywhere.

"Seeing the people, He felt compassion for them, because they were distressed and dispirited like sheep without a shepherd. Then He said to His disciples, 'The harvest is plentiful, but the workers are few. Therefore beseech the Lord of the harvest to send out workers into His harvest."[2]

Unfortunately, too many of us live with our heads buried in our phones, hurrying from one place to the next. Who has time for people?

Part of the awakening that happens when we GO is that our Father helps us look up and see people. People are hurting. People want to be noticed. People need to be heard. He gives us eyes for their brokenness that perhaps we haven't had before.

The ministry of noticing is incredible. Even in our fast-paced, technology-driven world, people find genuine questions refreshing.

When was the last time someone sincerely asked you how you were doing and actually listened? How did it make you feel? Sometimes the most natural way to share the love of Jesus with another soul comes from asking a simple question like "How are you doing?" and then listening. How hard is that?

As was true for Philip, God has "distressed and dispirited" people ahead on your highways and byways. Begin by praying.

- Actively trust Him with the issues you're dealing with each day. This will help get your eyes off you so you can see others.
- Ask Him to guide you to those He wants you to share with.
- Be open to the Spirit's leading. If He doesn't show you anyone to speak with today, then bless the Lord for His

---

[2] Matthew 9:36–38.

faithfulness. If He does, then notice what that person is doing. The Holy Spirit doesn't want to make this awkward for you or for the other person. Let Him guide your words and steps. Speak. And be faithful to share whatever the Spirit leads you to say. Remember, you are merely being faithful.

In the eyes of strangers, the circumstances bringing you and this person together may seem bizarre. Who are you to say something to him or her? Why would that individual ever care about what you have to say? *But in the Spirit, you have words of LIFE! And you have an appointment with this person scheduled by God Himself!*

As you learn to relax in the Spirit's leading, you'll have regular opportunities to share with others. Your adventure in GO-ing isn't to make a list of all the people you lead to the Lord. You may only lead one person in your lifetime—or you may lead hundreds. Who knows.

God knows.

Through His Spirit, He has appointments for you to keep with people who, like the Ethiopian, may not understand spiritual things, but with God's help, you'll be there to listen and help them on their journey.

YOUR PEOPLE

Bobby Herring, street name Tre9, leads Eyes On Me, a Houston-based ministry that mentors, disciples, and serves at-risk youth and their families. One of Bobby's approaches is to start churches in apartment complexes. He and his team go door-to-door, sharing the love of Jesus, looking for receptive hearts. When someone surrenders to the Lord, that person becomes a part of the church in their complex.

Among the many interesting aspects of Bobby's story is that he is white but the place where he ministers, Houston's Fifth Ward, is brown and black. I am fascinated by how people find fields in which to minister. So I asked Bobby how his heart was turned on to this particular demographic. He replied, "Because that's where I grew up. I grew up in an inner-city, predominantly brown and black community. Moody Park. Sam Houston High School."[3] The Holy Spirit sent Bobby back to the people from which he came.

As we have seen, the Samaritan woman who surrendered to Jesus in John 4 immediately went back to her people and began telling them her Jesus story. When Jesus began His public ministry, the first people He went to were the Jews. Because He was one of them, He had access to them that non-Jewish people would not so easily have.

In the book of Acts, both Peter and Paul went to Jews first, sharing Jewish stories. In Acts 2, when Peter stood to give his first public sermon, he preached on the day of Pentecost,[4] a Jewish celebration of the early barley harvest and the giving of the Torah (the first five books of the Bible) on Mount Sinai. His sermon identified Old Testament prophecies about the coming Messiah

---

[3] From an interview with the author on September 25, 2020.
[4] The word *Pentecost* comes from the Greek and means "fifty." This holiday occurs fifty days after Easter, commemorating the descent of the Holy Spirit on the apostles and the birth of the early church. The Jewish people also celebrate *Shavuot*, which is fifty days after Passover.

as Jesus. Jesus was their long-awaited fulfillment! A Gentile, not having been raised with the expectation of a Messiah, would not have understood or appreciated what Peter was saying.

Similarly, in Paul's three missionary journeys, he stopped in at least eleven places that we know of. At each stop, the first thing Paul did was go to the local synagogue or gathering of Jewish people. He went to his people first.

Acts 13:4–5 describes the pattern: "Being sent out by the Holy Spirit, they went down to Seleucia and from there they sailed to Cyprus. When they reached Salamis, they began to proclaim the word of God in the synagogues of the Jews." Having been saved out of Judaism, Paul returned to the Jewish people, telling the story of Jesus to reach the lost.

God often demonstrates in Scripture that the first people He wants us to share with are the groups we already belong to. Shortly after giving my life to Jesus, I started a Bible study at my workplace. I have no idea if I "should" have been leading the study or not. I just knew Jesus loved my co-workers, and these were "my" people. I didn't tell them Jesus was the Messiah; that would have meant nothing to them. I told them Jesus loved them and had life for them.

I worked out at a gym for six years. Before I joined, I asked the Lord to send me to the gym where the people were that He wanted me to reach. I can work out anywhere. I wanted to go wherever He wanted me going. And you know what? He didn't lead me to start a Bible study at the gym; instead, He led me to build relationships with people. Over time, I prayed with many of the men and women there, even seeing one man healed of an ankle injury.

These people became "my" people. I earned credibility with them that opened up gospel opportunities.

I'm most comfortable talking with people about Jesus over breakfast, coffee, or lunch. I love the one-on-one dialogue. So I regularly ask "my" people to share a meal. Typically, the Spirit directs the conversation by creating an opportunity for me to share my story. Since I'm with somebody I already have a connection with, the transition is super comfortable and easy. Who doesn't want to hear about the story of someone they know?

Who are your people? Where did you come from? In what circles do you travel? How is God our Father preparing the way for you to share your story with them? Make a list of your people who don't know Jesus. Begin praying for them. Ask the Lord to create opportunities for you to share with them. Invite them to a meal. Be ready for the Holy Spirit to guide the conversation. Then, use your story in your language and your way that speaks to your people.

In these conversations, you'll get questions you don't know the answer to. Don't be afraid. There's no way you could have every answer no matter who you are. Simply say an appropriate form of "That's a great question. Let me find out the answer and get back to you." Let the Holy Spirit work, and watch what He will do through you!

MISSION TRIPS

The Big Feed is an annual event in Matamoros, Mexico, hosted by Way of the Cross, the ministry led by Ben Butler (see chapter 4). The event feeds more than 10,000 people in a day. The field is covered with people; there are games and giveaways. For several years, Way of the Cross gave away a house! The center of the event is the main stage, where all throughout the day the gospel is preached.

I can't remember how many times I've been to the Big Feed, but it's more than ten. I started going a couple of years after I gave my life to Jesus.

Through my relationship with Ben and Way of the Cross, I began doing mission work in Nicaragua. I have been there almost twenty times. What started out as crusade ministry—where we would host four different events a day preaching the gospel and handing out food—became a relationship with one church in Jinotega. Pastor Oscar Perez and his congregation at Hebron Baptist Church have become family.

Through another connection, I went to Addis Ababa, Ethiopia, for appointment sharing (going to people's homes where our team had preset appointments) and church training.

Through a separate connection with Rick Peters Ministries, I've been to Cuba three times.

Foreign missions have profoundly impacted my confidence and my understanding of myself as a missionary and my life as a mission field. I've seen different approaches to gospel sharing. I've seen rejection and success. I've learned the importance of culture. I've seen healings and exorcisms. I prayed in the house of a witch for the healing of her daughter. I've seen the love our Father has for ALL people. And I have also seen that people—no matter the race, ethnicity, gender, education level, and so on—are just people. They want to be loved. They want to eat. They want to have hope. They have family issues. Their marriages are hard. They hurt for their kids. And they need Jesus. God our Father absolutely uses mission trips to reach people and to shape the hearts and lives of those on mission teams.

For those to whom the Holy Spirit leads you, you need to go. GO-ing has nothing to do with whether you have the "right" personality (whatever that is), the "right" experience (whatever that is), or the "right" amount of money (whatever that is). GO-ing simply involves being obedient to what the Holy Spirit is leading you to do. The foreign mission field can be an excellent training ground for highways and byways success.

FROM 10,000 TO 1

One year I took my friend Luis to the Big Feed. He had never been to this incredible event and was highly skeptical of the whole affair. *Offer down-and-out people food, and ask them if they want to surrender to Jesus, and of course they are going to raise their hands.* That's what he was thinking.

Ironically, we were talking about the legitimacy of what he was witnessing as we stood in the middle of 10,000 people. Luis tells the story from his perspective:

> We were debating. I said, with a rather flippant tone, "What? I'm supposed to just walk up to some random person and say, 'Hey, do you know Jesus?'"
>
> You said, "Not exactly. The Lord puts the people in your path that He is calling; it's not you calling them."
>
> I said, again rather flippantly, "Okay, then how do you know who to walk up to?"

You said, "I don't know. That's a matter of discernment. You have to be led to them."

That was not the answer I was looking for, so in order to prove the absurdity of the methodology, I scoffingly stopped the next kid (probably twelve years old) walking by and abruptly said, "Do you know Jesus?"

"No."

I repeated the question, incredulous that he didn't know who Jesus was, and the kid repeated, "No."

So I explained Jesus to him.

He replied, "Okay, and . . . ?"

So I delivered "the line" [an altar call kind of thing]. With some enthusiasm he responded, we prayed together for his salvation, I gave the "next line"—find a church, etc. We then shook hands, and he departed with a sparkle in his eye and a pep in his step.

I turned around and you were laughing, and I was blush red.

Luis has been a believer in the effectiveness of mission trips ever since! And his ministry in his highways and byways was forever changed!

God our Father has people for you to reach. Wonderfully led by the perfect fishing Guide, you'll be directed by the Holy Spirit to the 10 percent water where 90 percent of the fish are. Whether He sends you to "royalty," to the people you grew up with, or to those in another part of the world, He has people for you. Your effectiveness is not determined by your personality, the smoothness of your speech, or the depth of your theology. Your effectiveness is determined by your faithfulness to God's leading.

Imagine your success in fishing if you just listen to Kris Culpepper. Find the fish in the 10 percent of the rich waters. God our Father will send you there. Simply listen, notice, and GO. You'll be successful in reaching people if you will pray and respond to the Holy Spirit.

Chapter Work: 90/10

1. One of the struggles in effective flexing is finding the right people with whom to share. Thankfully, the Holy Spirit is our Father's perfect fishing guide. How does His leadership affect your confidence to share? Spend time in prayer asking the Holy Spirit to give you assurance of His presence and leading in your evangelism. Rest in Him. What images, Scripture passages, or songs come to mind?

2. What are the challenges you have in listening to and obeying the Holy Spirit as He leads you to share with others? Preoccupation with one's issues is a common obstacle to effective listening. List the internal issues you are battling today that have you preoccupied with your life and that hinder you from seeing others. After listing them, pray through each one, declaring that our Father is faithful.

3. Take a moment and focus on two groups of people. One group is friends, family, neighbors, and co-workers. List at least ten people from this first group who do not know Jesus and begin praying for opportunities to share Jesus with them. Like the woman at the well, the second group is people you will meet in your highways and byways. At the beginning of each day, pray and ask the Holy Spirit to tune you into His leading to share with anyone He has in your path today.

4. What are the obstacles you face in interacting with non-Christians? Write each of them down. Then, ask our Father to give you whatever is needed—wisdom, breakthrough, something else—so that you can have regular sharing opportunities.

8 The Biology of Rejection

Your body has two adrenal glands. They are shaped like triangles and located on top of your kidneys. When you perceive a situation as stressful or fearful, your brain alerts your nervous system, which signals your adrenal glands to release adrenaline into your bloodstream. Your heart rate increases. Your breath becomes shallow. There's an increase of oxygen to your brain. And your senses go on high alert. This is commonly called the "fight-or-flight response."

I like to choose the "flight" option when my wife wants me to ride really tall roller coasters.

Many of us have the same biological response anytime we consider sharing Jesus. Our minds imagine a multitude of stress-inducing scenarios where others are going to reject us, think we're weird, or respond in another negative way. These thoughts trigger our adrenals to dump adrenaline. We give in to the fear and flee rather than becoming the fishers of men Jesus invited us to be.

The fear is real.

The biology is real.

But "flight" doesn't have to be our response. In the power of the Holy Spirit, we can deny our fear and faithfully GO as our Father leads.

Many people miss out on God's plan because of fear. They know He has a plan for their lives. They know He can do miraculous work. All they have to do is stand firm.

Nope. Fear.

They're afraid our Father *will not* deliver.

Or afraid they won't like *what* He delivers.

Or afraid they won't like *when* He delivers.

Or afraid the other person will *reject* what He delivers.

Fear can be a powerful weapon against faith.

At the time of his death, Moses was the greatest leader in the history of Israel. God used him to deliver the Hebrew people from Egyptian captivity (Egypt was the dominant world power at that time). God performed amazing miracles through Moses and gave him the Ten Commandments. Moses was respected and revered by his people. No one was like him.[1]

And then he died. And it was time for a new leader.

God replaced Moses with a man named Joshua. Can you imagine the pressure? Have you ever had to follow a beloved leader? How could Joshua ever compare?

Four times, God's word came to Joshua: "Be strong and courageous."[2] This was not a neat phrase for a T-shirt, or something

---

[1] Deuteronomy 34:10.
[2] Deuteronomy 31:7; Joshua 1:6, 9, 18.

to be hung on a wall or retweeted. God knew this new role would provide many opportunities for Joshua's adrenal glands to dump adrenaline into his bloodstream. He knew Joshua would be confronted with fight-or-flight thoughts, and He wanted to embolden Joshua to stand firm in those times and be faithful.

Joshua stood on the eastern bank of the Jordan River. All Israel was behind him, watching. He needed to lead his people across and to the other side. God told him to step in. Once he did, God would part the waters.

I imagine Joshua's fear. His adrenals were pumping. I'm sure he was thinking, *Is this going to work? I'm not Moses.*

What if God doesn't come through? I'm going to look like an idiot in front of the entire nation.

Why me? There has to be another way.

These thoughts were probably bombarding his mind like debris being tossed in a hurricane.

But God gave Joshua the assurance, "Be strong and courageous," to invoke in these specific scenarios. Crossing the Jordan was part of God's calling and mission in Joshua's life. God waited to see if Joshua would trust Him, deny his desire to flee, and step into the water. As Joshua obeyed, God supplied:

> When those who carried the ark came into the Jordan, and the feet of the priests carrying the ark were dipped in the edge of the water . . . the waters which were flowing down from above stood and rose up in one heap. . . . And the priests who carried the ark of the covenant of the LORD stood firm on dry ground in the middle of the Jordan while all Israel crossed

on dry ground, until all the nation had finished crossing the Jordan.[3]

We don't have to run just because our adrenals are telling us to. Like Joshua, we can learn to deny our flight impulses, be strong and courageous despite our fear, and succeed in whatever God is leading us to do.

When you share Jesus with another person, there are only three possible responses they can have: yes, no, or maybe. Envision the one you're sharing with saying, "YES, I would like to follow Jesus!" How would that make you feel? What depth of joy would you have? How exciting would that be? I assume you're not afraid of this happening!

Now envision that individual answering with some version of "Maybe, but not right now." They want more information. They need more time. They want to be in a different place. Whatever their reason, they responded well to you; they just didn't say yes. Still, they're open to getting together again. How great would you feel at God using you to plant a seed in a person's life, knowing that someone else may harvest it? Again, I assume this scenario doesn't stir up fear in you.

Now, here comes the dreaded "no." Being told no is the scenario that creates all the fear. And it's not just being told no—it's the manner in which someone might say no that scares us. Envision someone politely responding to you, "No thanks, I'm not interested." How does that make you feel? Though you don't

---

[3] Joshua 3:15–17.

love that response, it's not adrenal-dumping, must-run-away negative either.

So, most of our fear comes from scenarios in which people respond with some degree of hostility. The picture of someone yelling at us or calling us names is what paralyzes us. Let's press into those fears about the harsh no and see what the Holy Spirit can do to alleviate them. God doesn't want this to be an anxiety-producing nightmare. He wants us to delight in the great privilege of sharing the words of life with others! And, He wants us to experience the thrill of co-laboring with Him to create new life.

FEAR OF REJECTION

Did you know that the most common fear in the world—more than heights, spiders, and snakes—is the fear of social rejection? The thought of being rejected by someone can be terrifying. Paralyzing. It can easily make us feel that we're not good enough. That we have some fundamental flaw and are broken.

Like pulling the emergency brake on a car, the fear of rejection can immediately and forcefully stop a person from sharing Jesus.

There must be some solution, because God our Father is not cruel. He is not bent on torturing His children who are bound up in this fear by forcing them to be rejected. I cannot imagine God demanding that I, with my fear of heights, walk out on a two-foot-wide bridge, 2,000 feet above the ground, saying, "If you love Me, you'll cross this bridge."

God sends us to GO, not as feeble people who have suffered a lifetime of rejection, but as His sons and daughters, adopted and filled up with the love and encouragement of His family. How is this possible? How can someone who's afraid of rejection be transformed into a person at rest in the Lord?

Through love and understanding. The love of Jesus and His people are a soothing balm to wounded souls. Meanwhile, understanding gives us wisdom to see the bigger picture of rejection in a way that can transform our experience.

The Balm of Love. For the one who has been continually made to feel worthless, the love of Jesus can heal. Jesus ministers as we allow Him into our fear and into the wounds that have caused that fear. Rejection feels terrible. And the fear of rejection—walking around with worry and anxiety that the next person you talk with could make you feel unworthy again—is miserable. Jesus wants to heal those wounds so that you can enjoy your new life, your new reality, in Him.

He begins His healing work in us by re-creating us.

When a person surrenders their life to Jesus, the Holy Spirit enters them and re-creates them. The apostle Paul wrote, "If anyone is in Christ, he is a new creature; the old things passed away; behold, new things have come."[4] Part of what has passed away is the old ways by which we valued ourselves. Before Jesus, we derived our worth—good or bad—primarily through the eyes of our parents and, secondarily, through society, the messages of the world. If our parents rejected us or praised us, if the world said we do or don't look right, act right, or have the right things, that is how we valued ourselves.

BUT.

---

[4] 2 Corinthians 5:17.

In Jesus, ALL of that changes. Whereas we lived in bondage to the dictionary of our parents or our culture, in Christ we now live in freedom according to His values. His words about us supersede EVERY word that doesn't align with His! Culture defines blessing by money and toys. Jesus defines blessing by intimacy with Him and faithfulness to Him. One is right; the other is wrong.

Therefore, when anyone comes to faith, their dictionary changes. Who they look to and what they believe about themselves *must* convert. Any word, name, thought, or feeling that doesn't align with Jesus *must* be rejected. "See how great a love the Father has bestowed on us, that we would be called children of God; and such we are"[5] will become the new value statement for every person who calls on the name of the Lord. This is the transformational glory of LIFE in Jesus!

As the one who has been held captive by rejection rests in their new identity as a child of God (a value statement that is grounded in the indwelling presence of the Holy Spirit and acceptance of God the Father), internal change begins. And their new personal value gets confirmed through the love and affection of other followers of Jesus.

Families of origin can be sources of great pain. Dads can be abusive. Moms can be negligent. Biological families are often clueless about the truth of who we are in Jesus, and thus they don't build us up. But Jesus intended for His people to be a new family, providing healthy, loving relationships.

---

[5] 1 John 3:1.

Jesus said, "Truly I say to you, there is no one who has left house or brothers or sisters or mother or father or children or farms, for My sake and for the gospel's sake, but that he will receive a hundred times as much now in the present age, houses and brothers and sisters and mothers and children and farms, along with persecutions; and in the age to come, eternal life."[6]

Paul explained that the way we talk to each other as family members of God our Father should build up each person: "Let no unwholesome word proceed from your mouth, but only such a word as is good for edification according to the need of the moment, so that it will give grace to those who hear."[7] Our new family is intended to be a place of love and encouragement, a place of healing from the wounds of rejection.

God's family is never perfect. Unfortunately, many of us also have been wounded by those in the church. We can ourselves be guilty of hurting others. In the body of Christ, grace, mercy, and forgiveness must be regular practices. Though we still fail, we walk together with Christ out of our own brokenness and mutual desire to love each other as He first loved us. And in the Spirit, we become family, experiencing our value through those whom God supplies as spiritual fathers, mothers, brothers, and sisters. Now we are able to GO, not as feeble people who have suffered a lifetime of rejection, but as men and women of God who've been adopted into His family and are being healed and filled up with the love and encouragement of our new family.

---

[6] Mark 10:29–30.
[7] Ephesians 4:29.

The Balm of Understanding. In addition to the balm of love is understanding. Through understanding we gain insight into what's really going on when we are rejected. We need to embrace the truth that rejection in evangelism is not personal. Like dating someone whose parents have rejected every other person their son or daughter has ever been in a relationship with, you are not being rejected because of you. You are being rejected because of Jesus in you.

Jesus explained, "The one who listens to you listens to Me, and the one who rejects you rejects Me; and he who rejects Me rejects the One who sent Me."[8] That's a lot of rejection!

But look carefully at what He said.

First, when you share, you are not alone. Jesus and the Father are there with you. Second, when you are rejected, you are not alone. While you are being rejected, Jesus and God the Father are being rejected as well. Rejection in Jesus is different. You may *feel* alone, as if there is something wrong with you. Yet you are being rejected not because you're foolish or defective but because you are offering Jesus.

Let's observe a scenario in which you are sharing the gospel with someone. You are sharing in the fullness—the presence and power—of the person of the Holy Spirit, in the will of our Father, and in the name of Jesus. You are not alone. You're on the winning team. You are not a loser holding a loser's hand. You have the map to hidden treasure, the secret formula to LIFE, the key to the door of heaven!

---

[8] Luke 10:16.

It's like you're offering that person a filet mignon prepared by a master chef. While you didn't cook it, you have tasted the chef's filet before and you can verify: it's amazing! Yet the person rejects you. Calls you a name. Knocks the filet out of your hands. You are being rejected, but even more, the chef is being rejected. How do you feel? Do you take this personally? You know what the person is missing. Instead of feeling broken because they rejected you, you feel sad for what they're missing, don't you?

I'm not understating or ignoring the fear of rejection. The fear of it is very powerful and subtle in the ways it affects us. I don't believe most people are healed of that fear instantly (although God can certainly deliver people from fear as He wishes). I do believe the fear of rejection is most strongly dealt with by regularly soaking in Trinitarian love and refuting the lies and imaginings that don't conform to God's truth.

In *BE: The Way of Rest*, I wrote about the discipline of reflecting. When we reflect on and soak in the truths of God, we're allowing the Holy Spirit to align our thoughts, feelings, and lives with our heavenly Father's. We are changed, and we learn to live in the continual flow of our Father's words. If the fear of rejection has a deep hold on you, please consider allowing someone who is skilled by the Holy Spirit to help restore you to freedom. Spirit-gifted counselors can do amazing ministry in this way. Pray that our Father will lead you to the right counselor for you. Ask your pastor or a trusted Christian friend to recommend one.

The fear of rejection, while powerful enough to paralyze our faithfulness to share Jesus, is not more powerful than the love and restoration of the Holy Spirit.

FEAR OF PERSECUTION

Part of my jiujitsu training was learning self-defense. Whether I was being attacked with punches, knives, chairs, or guns, I needed to defend myself.

Obviously, we cannot control how we may be attacked, but we can be prepared. Before jiujitsu, the thought of being assaulted by someone produced fear in me. I didn't want to get hit, much less stabbed. However, the more I trained, the less fear I felt. I still don't want to get hit or stabbed, but now I'm prepared should the situation present itself.

Persecution comes in many forms—you can be emotionally persecuted, where you're heckled or called names; you can be socially persecuted, getting kicked out of or shunned by a group; you can be physically persecuted by being beaten or incarcerated, or by someone damaging or taking your property. But when we allow Christ into our fear of persecution, He can strengthen us so that we're prepared should the situation present itself.

Our Father wants to send us into the world, not as timid people who are afraid of what may happen to us, but as sons and daughters strengthened and empowered by the Holy Spirit, and as men and women whose lives are held in the mighty hand of God. Jesus never shied away from warning of the very real dangers of walking with Him. He never watered down the world's enmity toward Him or Satan's hatred for Him. On the contrary, He regularly prepared His followers for what they would suffer because of Him.

His life experience proved His teaching on the reality of persecution:

- His hometown did not accept Him.[9]
- People in small towns kicked him out.[10]
- A member of His team, Judas Iscariot, betrayed Him.[11]
- Another member of His team, Peter, denied he ever knew Him.[12]
- Jewish leaders in the city of Jerusalem tried to stone Him,[13] plotted His death,[14] incited a mob against Him, and had Him executed.[15]
- And a Roman governor ordered His beating and crucifixion.[16]

Like Jesus, the apostle Paul endured all forms of persecution as well. He listed some of the things he suffered in 2 Corinthians 11:23–27:

> . . . in far more labors, in far more imprisonments, beaten times without number, often in danger of death. Five times I received from the Jews thirty-nine lashes. Three times I was beaten with rods, once I was stoned, three times I was shipwrecked, a night and a day I have spent in the deep. I have been on frequent journeys, in dangers from rivers, dangers from robbers, dangers from my countrymen, dangers from

---

[9] Luke 4:16–30.
[10] Luke 8:37.
[11] Matthew 26:14–16.
[12] Matthew 26:69–75.
[13] John 8:59.
[14] John 11:47–53.
[15] Luke 23:13–25.
[16] Matthew 27:24–31.

the Gentiles, dangers in the city, dangers in the wilderness, dangers on the sea, dangers among false brethren; I have been in labor and hardship, through many sleepless nights, in hunger and thirst, often without food, in cold and exposure.

His experience in persecution led him to prepare Timothy, a pastor who Paul poured his life into, with these words: "Indeed, all who desire to live godly in Christ Jesus will be persecuted."[17]

All of this can feel overwhelming! The reality of persecution is not a great sales pitch for energizing people to go and share Jesus with others.

How can anyone survive this? And why would anyone want to? *Love.*

Strong in Love. Jesus endured all forms of persecution for this reason. He lived in the full love of the Father and the Holy Spirit. He entered the darkness of this world because He loved His Father and wanted to be faithful. He came to this earth because He loved you and me. When He looks at those who don't know Him, His heart is moved by love to reach them.

The Gospel of Luke says that on Palm Sunday, the day Jesus entered Jerusalem for His final week before being crucified, He saw the city and wept over it (19:41). His heart broke for the souls of men and women who did not believe. Jesus endured the false accusations, the beating, the torture of being hung on a cross because He knew His sacrifice would make it possible for any willing soul to be saved. This is how love endures persecution. In

---

[17] 2 Timothy 3:12.

1 John 4:10 we read: "In this is love, not that we loved God, but that He loved us and sent His Son to be the propitiation [the one who paid the penalty] for our sins."

Describing love in 1 Corinthians 13:4–7, Paul wrote, "Love . . . bears all things, believes all things, hopes all things, endures all things." Then he added in verse 13, "But now faith, hope, love, abide these three; but the greatest of these is love."

I love the Lord. The Lord loves me. As a result, I love all those He wants to reach through me. If I have to suffer for their salvation, then I go the way of Jesus, and the cost is worth it.

The power of love is greater than the pain of persecution.

How can anyone survive this? And why would anyone want to?

Supernatural strength.

Strong in the Lord. On their own, no one is strong enough to endure the headwinds of the world. But anyone surrendered to the power of the Holy Spirit can be made strong. We marvel at Paul's ability to endure what he suffered and think, *There's no way I could do that!* On his own, Paul *couldn't* do what he did. He's an excellent example of a man made strong in the Lord.

Paul wrote about his own experience with weakness:

> There was given me a thorn in the flesh, a messenger of Satan to torment me—to keep me from exalting myself! Concerning this I implored the Lord three times that it might leave me. And He has said to me, "My grace is sufficient for you, for power is perfected in weakness." Most gladly, therefore, I will rather boast about my weaknesses, so that the power of Christ may dwell in me. Therefore I am well content with weaknesses,

with insults, with distresses, with persecutions, with difficulties, for Christ's sake; for when I am weak, then I am strong.[18]

Notice how Paul's definition of strength was upended in the Lord. Paul defined strength as the ability to endure. True power—the power of God—flows through human weakness!

The world told Paul what it tells all of us: strength is found in being strong in yourself. Jesus taught that to be strong, you must be weak. So, Paul began boasting in his weakness—the very thing he feared before.

Be weak in the Lord. Be unable to endure. Be powerless to persevere. And, more than that, boast in it! Andrew Murray, a South African author and pastor who ministered in the late 1800s and early 1900s, wrote, "Man's chief care, his highest virtue, and his only happiness, now and throughout eternity, is to present himself as an empty vessel in which God can dwell and manifest His power and goodness."[19]

How can anyone survive this? And why would anyone want to?

Wisdom.

Strong in Wisdom. The book of 1 Peter is a manual on suffering well. Its message was needed because many Christians had been scattered due to persecution in Jerusalem. Peter wrote to equip fellow believers to suffer well.

Do not fear their intimidation, and do not be troubled, but sanctify Christ as Lord in your hearts, always being ready to

---

[18] 2 Corinthians 12:7–10.
[19] Andrew Murray, *Humility* (New Kensington, PA: Whitaker House, 1982), 16.

make a defense to everyone who asks you to give an account for the hope that is in you. (3:14–15)

Beloved, do not be surprised at the fiery ordeal among you, which comes upon you for your testing, as though some strange thing were happening to you; but to the degree that you share the sufferings of Christ, keep on rejoicing, so that also at the revelation of His glory you may rejoice with exultation. (4:12–14)

Be of sober spirit, be on the alert. Your adversary, the devil, prowls around like a roaring lion, seeking someone to devour. But resist him, firm in your faith, knowing that the same experiences of suffering are being accomplished by your brethren who are in the world. After you have suffered for a little while, the God of all grace, who called you to His eternal glory in Christ, will Himself perfect, confirm, strengthen and establish you. To Him be dominion forever and ever. Amen. (5:8–11)

Peter called all disciples of Christ to wisdom in suffering. The world is hostile toward Jesus, with satanic forces engaged in battle against Him and His people. As we continue to learn about and understand the severity of the war, we will be less and less surprised when persecution comes.

We can also draw strength from the wisdom of the "fellowship of suffering"—holding to hope because we know that brothers and sisters around the world and across time have also maintained hope amid persecution. Finally, those in Christ should be energized to endure by the knowledge of the glory that is to come. While the Christian may suffer here, eternal rejoicing waits for the one who endures.

NEVER ALONE

Preacher and evangelist John Wesley was riding along a road one day when it dawned on him that three whole days had passed in which he had suffered no persecution. Not a brick or an egg had been thrown at him. Alarmed, he stopped his horse and exclaimed, "Can it be that I have sinned, and am backslidden?"

Climbing off the saddle, Wesley went down on his knees and began interceding with God to show him where he might be at fault. A rough fellow on the other side of the hedge, hearing the prayer, looked across and recognized the preacher. "I'll fix that Methodist preacher," he said, picking up a brick and tossing it over at him. It missed its mark and fell harmlessly beside Wesley. Whereupon Wesley leaped to his feet, joyfully exclaiming, "Thank God, it's all right. I still have His presence."[20]

So, envision a scenario in which you suffer some form of persecution. Do not see yourself as being alone. As God was with Joseph in the pit, David on the battlefield against Goliath, Daniel in the lions' den, Esther in front of King Ahasuerus, Stephen when he was stoned, Peter in prison, and Jesus on the cross, He will be with you. None of us can hold up under persecution on our own. No one is tough enough. But in the Holy Spirit, we are empowered to stand firm and persevere.

---

[20] Paul Lee Tan, *Encyclopedia of 7,700 Illustrations: Signs of the Times* (Garland, TX: Bible Communications, Inc., 1996), 995.

Whether persecution comes via emotional or physical harm, disassociation, imprisonment, or death, it is a real and powerful threat that can keep us from sharing Jesus with others if left unchecked. But in the awesome might of the Holy Spirit, we are not bound by our fears. In Him and through Him we can walk in victory, renouncing our fears, drawing strength from the Lord's exhortation to "be strong and courageous," and engaging with others in ways we never thought we could!

What fears or hesitations do you have? What is keeping you from joyfully, freely sharing the love of Jesus with others? Will you bring those fears to your Father in heaven? If you're not sure what's holding you back, let Him make those concerns known to you. Let Him replace your issues with dreams and visions of His truth, and of you as a missionary. Let the Holy Spirit show you how completely He is with you.

Be still. Renounce your adrenaline-fueled desire to flee the scene. And then GO.

BY FAITH, NOT FEAR

Tim is fifty-four years old. He runs his own staffing company, sourcing talent for organizations. Like many whose faith is formed from different streams, he was raised Catholic and became a Methodist after marrying his Baptist wife.

Tim has powerfully witnessed God's faithfulness over the past five years as he has worked with people in recovery. Three months ago, Tim read the book *Imagine Heaven* by John Burke.[21] In the

---

[21] John Burke, *Imagine Heaven: Near-Death Experiences, God's Promises, and the Exhilarating Future That Awaits You* (Grand Rapids, MI: Baker, 2015).

book, Burke describes the numerous near-death experiences that others have reported. Many of their experiences include similar elements. But while most people see some form of bright light that they experience as love, some encounter demonic darkness.

God our Father used this book to crystallize for Tim the beauty of what is to come and a fear for where he does not want to go. My friend's fire for sharing Jesus was lit. Every opportunity he gets, Tim shares the gospel or sends a copy of *Imagine Heaven*. "I have shared Jesus more in the past two to three months than I have in my entire life," Tim recently said to me. "People need to know the life that is for us in Jesus."

The dad of one of Tim's clients passed away in December of 2019. That client's wife divorced him the next month, and in February 2020, the man's son died. Then the pandemic hit in March. What does one say to him?

On our own, it's almost impossible to have any words. But God our Father strategically placed Tim in this man's life. The Holy Spirit had prepared him for this. Tim faithfully stepped into this man's tragedy, sat with him in his grief, and, when appropriate, shared the five-star, lifesaving, transformational love of Jesus.

No matter where you are in life, fear doesn't have to control you. It doesn't have to keep you from living the abundant life of Jesus or sharing the love of Jesus with others. God our Father sees you! He instills the fire of the Holy Spirit in you! He waits for you to trust Him, to come to Him in your weaknesses, fears, and doubts so He can send you in His power to be a force of love in the lives of many.

Chapter Work:
The Biology of Rejection

Fear is a powerful weapon used against us to keep us from effectively sharing Jesus with others. In your journal, or on a piece of paper, use this chart to help identify your specific fears, and then receive our Father's assurance just as He gave assurance to Joshua (Joshua 1:7).

Fear	Lie	Truth	Assurance

Take comfort. You are not alone in your fears. As you allow the Holy Spirit to minister to you, He will wonderfully heal you and give you the assurance you need to walk in His power, clarity, and boldness.

May our Father continue to work in you by His Holy Spirit so that you can fulfill Jesus' invitation to you: "Follow Me, and I will make you become fishers of men" (Mark 1:17).

EPILOGUE: The Adventure

This is an excellent time to take a big, deep breath.

Go ahead, take a minute to breathe deeply in and out.

We've covered a lot of ground together. And we have wrestled with many things. Our Father's love for you in Jesus is deeper and wider than you know or understand. He has gone to great lengths to adopt you. He planned the steps of your salvation before you knew what He was doing. With the same expertise, He has planned the steps of your life in Him as well.

Along the way, He's been writing your story as only He could. He's been investing in you, teaching you, blessing you, drawing you to Himself, and restoring you. Now He wants to send you.

If sharing Jesus were easy and we all excelled at it, this book wouldn't be necessary. But so many of us struggle with sharing the Good News, and most of us will never do it. In the Lord, I want so much for you to know the depth of our Father's love so that you can be freed from everything that keeps you from GO-ing. I want you to be equipped, energized, and excited to flex your story

EPILOGUE: THE ADVENTURE

power as the Holy Spirit leads. I want you to be so taken by Jesus that you tell everyone, "I have a guy! . . ."

My friend Bobby Herring (see chapter 7) recently said: "I need to go get my adventure on!" I love that.

Walking in the Holy Spirit is a daily adventure. The same Holy Spirit who drove all the action in the book of Acts waits to write you into others' stories.

If you are in Christ, you have a five-star life. You may need to spend some time remembering your story. You may need to ask the Holy Spirit to remind you of key details and people that have been part of your journey. That's a good thing. Our Father wants you to share with others from the overflow of what He has done and is doing in you.

Take some time to think about the specific blessings you experience. You may not need three; just one can be awesome. But get that one clearly in mind. Practice sharing it. Connect it to Scripture.

And remember, you are not alone. Sharing is not golf. The Holy Spirit of the living God is in you. You walk in the undefeatable will of our Father. And you share the good news of Jesus, who is by far the greatest man who ever lived. You are a winning part of THE winning team!

When you get roughed up, take it to the Lord. Hear Jesus say to you through the Holy Spirit, "I know, and I am with you." When you fail, take it to the Lord. Hear our Father say, "You're in training. You walk by grace." Listen as He gives you lessons on how you could have handled a situation differently. He wants you to succeed!

GO: FLEX YOUR STORY POWER

Hopefully your eyes have been opened a little more to just how much your friends, neighbors, and co-workers need Jesus. I don't care how attractive or together their lives look on the outside; internally, they are dealing with their brokenness. The systems of this world do . . . not . . . work. Satan is on the prowl, destroying life everywhere. Abundant life and eternal life hang in the balance. Continue to learn how to see people as Jesus sees them: distressed and dispirited. And then be faithful to go as He sends, because "the harvest is plentiful, but the workers are few."[1]

Most people you talk to will say no. A portion of those who say no will reject you. A smaller portion will persecute you. Yet love will carry you. The cause of Christ will empower you.

Some will say maybe, looking forward to future opportunities to explore faith with you. And then some will say yes! For those who do, God our Father will use you to change the eternal trajectory of their soul. You will feel indescribable joy at their salvation and be flooded with new hope at witnessing this miracle of spiritual birth.

And that, my friends, is awesome.

May God our Father fill every one of us with courage, boldness, passion, and energy as we flex our story power, imparting life to others through Jesus' love. As we GO to make disciples, may we experience the fulfillment of this incredible promise from Jesus in Matthew 28:20:

"I am with you always, even to the end of the age."

---

[1] Matthew 9:37.

ANOTHER BOOK BY JIM STERN

BE:
THE WAY OF REST
BY JIM STERN | TREXO.ORG

"The discipleship teaching and equipping that Jim shares is tear-evoking, eye-opening, and transforming for those who have ears to hear and eyes to see. What Jim brings as a gift to the Body of Christ and those seeking a new life is nothing less than life-altering through the power of the Holy Spirit."

— Kathy Vosburg

BE A PART OF THE JOURNEY
Available from our website, TREXO.ORG, or Amazon.com

ANOTHER BOOK BY JIM STERN

BRILLIANT

Unleashing
LIFE
Through The
LORD'S PRAYER

"JIM'S TEACHING BRINGS CLARITY TO THE LORD'S PRAYER THAT HELPED ME BETTER APPRECIATE THE RICHNESS AND POWER OF THE WORDS JESUS SPOKE. I RECOMMEND *BRILLIANT* NOT AS JUST ANOTHER PRAYER BOOK BUT A WAY FOR US TO GAIN HOPE AND INTIMACY AS WE PRAY JESUS'S PRAYER."

–TAMI HEIM
PRESIDENT/CEO, CHRISTIAN LEADERSHIP ALLIANCE

Available from our website, TREXO.ORG, or Amazon.com

MAKE:
FALL 2021

COMING SOON
Visit our website, TREXO.ORG, for more details

TREXO
BY *Jim Stern*
TREXO.ORG

Unleashing The Power Of Personal Discipleship

STAY CONNECTED TO JIM STERN AND THE TREXO COMMUNITY